Be Your Own Boss

*For my twin sister Ethel and my brothers
Lincoln and John Paul.*

THE SUNDAY TIMES

Be Your Own Boss

THIRD EDITION

David McMullan

KOGAN PAGE | *CREATING SUCCESS*

First published in 1994
Second edition 1997
Third edition 2002, reprinted 2003

Kogan Page Limited
120 Pentonville Road
London N1 9JN

www.kogan-page.co.uk

British Library Cataloguing in Publication Data

A CIP record for this book is available from the British Library.

ISBN 0 7494 3884 3

Typeset by Saxon Graphics Ltd, Derby
Printed and bound in Great Britain by Clays Ltd, St Ives plc

contents

1. personal assessment   1
   changing for the better 2; the right frame of mind to
   succeed 3; are you right for self-employment? 4; self-
   assessment 6; working from home: the family
   implications 11; action 12; training and hard work 14;
   'let's not overthink this, let's just do it' 14

2. which business?   16
   buying an existing business 16; franchises 17; direct
   selling 20; researching your business idea 21; the product
   or service – is it right? 21; pricing 25; place 30;
   promotion 30

3. professional advice   33
   government help for new businesses 34; help for younger
   entrepreneurs 37; trade associations 37; other sources of
   information 39; questions to ask advisers 41

4. the business plan   42
   purpose of the business plan 42; format of the business
   plan 42; an example of a business plan 45; overheads
   budget 51; sales turnover 54; profit and loss account 54;
   cash flow forecast 56

5. raising finance   61
    yourself 62; your business partners 63; your spouse or
    life partner 63; parents, relatives or friends 63; loans 64;
    bank loans 64; the bank in perspective 66; finance
    companies 67; building societies 68; venture capital 68;
    government and European Union schemes and grants 69;
    the Prince's Youth Business Trust 69; credit unions 70

6. setting up: the business structure   73
    sole trader 73; partnership 75; the limited company 78;
    cooperatives 80; value added tax 81; useful sources of
    information 82

7. premises   84
    working from home 84; location 85; an answering service
    or a business centre? 86; retail premises 87; leasing
    premises 90; buying premises 91; local authorities,
    councils and development organisations 93; useful
    reference points to help with your search 95

8. marketing, selling and promotion   96
    prior to start date 97; advertising 98; using local papers
    100; the importance of selling 101; the mailshot 102;
    telephone selling 105; preparing for sales visits 116; the
    end of the selling week 123; development of existing
    accounts 124; your company image 125; customer care
    129; the Internet 130

9. managing the business   132
    managing your time 132; managing your cash flow 138;
    employing people 141; alternatives to employing people
    143; insurance 144; summary 145

10. sources of further information   146

acknowledgements

Special thanks go to Mr Barrie Moreton and the West Lancs Council for Voluntary Service for their support during the completion of this edition.

personal assessment

You probably already have an idea for being your own boss, but need to look at the ins and outs of setting up in business. This book is designed to help you do that.

To begin with, these are the kinds of question you need to ask and which this book will help you answer:

- Are you suited to being in business for yourself?
- How do you research your market?
- What do you charge?
- Do you need capital?
- How do you get capital, if you need it?
- How do you sell?
- How do you manage your time properly?
- What do you need to know about business bank accounts, yearly accounts and insurance?
- Do you need to be VAT registered?
- Should you set up as a sole trader, a partnership or a limited company?
- Where can you get advice, and is it free?

You will need to be business-minded and professional whether you are providing a service or a product, whether you are working from home or from business premises, whether you are a sole trader or a limited company and whether you intend to run your own business on a part-time or a full-time basis.

To that end, this book sets out to be practical and thorough, expecting to take nothing for granted.

changing for the better

The best sort of change is self-generated and self-driven. Individual change can be brought about only by individuals. *You* have to make the attempt, in this instance, to become *your* own boss.

Change can be treated as a threefold process. First, you project yourself on a mental plane into the life you want when it is changed. Second, you behave as if you have already undergone the desired change and are in the 'new' situation. Third, you metamorphose into the new situation. The boundaries dissolve and the change is in place.

The way others perceive you will have a strong effect on their willingness or otherwise to be of assistance – from the bank manager through to your first customer. You need to behave as though you were already a success in business.

Here are some useful pointers:

- You have between one and four minutes to make a good first impression. How you make that matters more than what you say.
- Fifty-five per cent is what others see, including body language.
- Thirty-eight per cent is what they hear, that is, tone of voice.
- Only 7 per cent is determined by the actual words used.

You represent your business. Continuous personal and professional development is essential to your success. Results do not yield themselves to those who refuse to give themselves fully to achieving the desired results.

the right frame of mind to succeed

A *positive attitude* in business translates into determination to adhere to your objectives without being deflected or discouraged. This means concentration, persistence and an eye for the main chance.

You have made the choice to be your own boss. Now clarify that objective. List what you see as positive about this choice on one piece of paper, and what you see as negative on another. Then discuss these with someone you trust. This will help avoid the 'floating anxiety' that may occur if you don't properly analyse and justify your choice.

Once you have clarified your objective, and thought yourself into the frame, trust your decision and go with it wholeheartedly. Throw your heart over the bar and your mind will follow.

Accept full responsibility for your choice and stay open as to what happens as a result: it may not lead in the direction expected. Review each stage continuously and modify as required so you remain flexible while staying on target.

Once you have faced up to your choice and carried it through to a conclusion, your confidence will improve and your frame of mind will adjust to being more positive.

Successful people are often perceived as being 'serious-minded', so you can be forgiven if you feel that you should stiffen up your manner. Yet having a good sense of humour is part and parcel of a positive approach. Not only does it help to keep stresses at bay, but a smile gives the impression of success by conveying the message that you, and therefore your company, are doing well.

If you can see your work as fun then you have latched on to an important component of the winning formula. Mood is important to performing a variety of tasks well. It makes sense to keep your sense of humour high on your list of goals.

To stay positive you will need to be physically fit. Mental fatigue is aggravated by an unhealthy body, and you will need energy aplenty as your own boss. Plan exercise into your schedule. This will re-energise your mind. It will also keep stress at bay.

A positive attitude must carry over into your general lifestyle so that your whole being becomes goal orientated. Being your own boss means that you have a duty to yourself to remain well. Absenting yourself from work means lost custom and credibility.

Keep in mind the TRAIN formula:

■ Talk about problems with someone who can help.
■ Relax each day – set aside time for this.
■ Activity, in the form of exercise, keeps stress at bay.
■ Interests beyond work allow you to recharge.
■ Nourish yourself – a good diet plus rewards for achievements.

Self-employment is a calling, not a job. It is attitude, not just aptitude, that helps determine your altitude. By making choices we define ourselves and carve out our own paths. In the final analysis you must simply *choose* to be successful. And that is a choice you must make as soon as you wake up each day.

are you right for self-employment?

What is motivating you to start up your own business? It might be one of the following:

1. You think it is better than being unemployed.
2. You want to make a lot of money.
3. You want to be your own boss.
4. You want job satisfaction.
5. You want to be other people's boss.
6. You want to join the fray and compete.

Look at these reasons more closely:

1. If this is your reason, then you are not one of what the Department of Employment (now the Department for Work and Pensions) used to call 'discouraged workers' who have given up trying to find a job, and that is good news. But you should assess your strengths very carefully as you may be taking 'Hobson's choice': accepting what you are getting rather than making a rational decision.

2. Look at the statistics again. If you are one of the new businesses that do ultimately succeed, that success may very well be the success of being able to sustain yourself and your family as a direct result of your own creativity. It is relative success, not necessarily monetary. Still, there is a great deal of satisfaction to be had in chasing money with a reasonable chance of overtaking it.

3. You will be your own boss. But this does not mean you are 'free'. You will probably be tied to the job more than you would be if you took the nine-to-five option. 'Freedom', at least at the outset, can mean hardship. Visit someone who already has their own business. It may cure you.

4. If you want the satisfaction of doing something different every day, you must realise that whatever you choose to do, there will be repetition involved. If you want the satisfaction of directing your own destiny you may be one of the lucky ones here. Generating your own income rewards you doubly, because it increases your self-esteem and your confidence.

5. The figures make for interesting reading. One source has it that two-thirds of new start-ups only employ themselves. Only 5.9 per cent of men employ more than 25 and only 3.6 per cent of women. If you want to be other people's boss, this is not the best route.

6. If you are genuinely competitive, you will certainly find enough to get excited about. If you can perceive hard, persistent work as simply 'competing', you've got a healthy focus. At the outset, it will not be unusual to spend two-thirds of your time looking for work and one-third actually doing it.

Now, having assessed anew your motivation for wishing to be your own boss, complete the following:

I want to be my own boss because _____

_____

self-assessment

What are your strengths and weaknesses, personal and financial? You will need to know these in order to build on sound foundations as you set off. It will help if you complete a simple questionnaire to establish a clear view of yourself before going any further.

It is important to decide first whether your financial position is such as will allow you to survive the early months of low or no income from the new venture.

personal finances

If you are in full-time employment now, it may be advisable to start your business on a part-time evening and weekend basis to test its feasibility. If you take this course, then add in your wage from your full-time job. Add in the income of your partner/spouse, if this is applicable.

There is no set profile for the individual who wants to be their own boss. You may be a student, a housewife, a tradesman or a manager who hankers after independence.

You may be of any age and either sex. You may have only the possibility of claiming on the Business Start-up Programme, or you may have £10,000 from an insurance policy that has paid off. There are various start-up initiatives – contact your local Business Link for details.

Many people start working for themselves after retirement – which nowadays may be as early as 55, for example in the fire service, or 50 if you have given 30 years' service. Such people may have finished paying off their mortgage, have a regular income from their pension, plus interest on savings. These so-called grey entrepreneurs account for approximately 15 per cent of all business start-ups in England and Wales, according to a Barclays Bank survey. This represents an increase of 50 per cent compared with a decade ago.

In the light of the possible variations, the following is a guideline to how you can assess your financial position. It can be modified to suit your particular circumstances.

Stage 1	**Monthly income £**
Wages monthly	_____
Wages monthly (partner/spouse)	_____
Child benefit	_____
Other state benefits, if applicable	_____
Interest on savings	_____
Other income: (eg, maintenance, rent)	_____
Subtotal	£ _____

Stage 2	**Monthly outgoings £**
Mortgage (or rent)	_____
Mortgage endowment policy	_____
Second mortgage	_____
Council tax (self and partner/spouse)	_____
Water rates	_____
Building/contents insurance	_____
House repairs/maintenance	_____

Life assurance _____
Pension policy _____
Electricity _____
Gas _____
Food _____
Milk bill _____
Window cleaner/gardener/cleaner _____
Cleaning materials _____
Other essentials _____
TV rental _____
TV licence _____
Maintenance payments _____
Nanny/au pair/childminder _____
School meals _____
Clothing _____
Telephone (home and mobile) _____
Car tax (road fund licence) _____
Car insurance _____
Petrol _____
Car maintenance _____
Other travelling expenses _____
Hire purchase, etc _____
Medicines _____
Toiletries _____
Hairdressing _____
Pets _____
Christmas, birthdays and holidays _____
Pocket money _____
Newspapers _____
Cigarettes _____
Outings _____
Sundry _____
Subtotal £_____

£

Stage 3

Total income (Stage 1)

Subtract total outgoings (Stage 2)

Available income total   £ _____

If the available income total is a minimal figure, you should ask yourself whether it is sensible to proceed. The best time to fire yourself is before you begin. You must assume there will be little or no income in the first half-year from your new venture. What will you survive on?

If you are unemployed, you still need to draw up a budget planner. You may be eligible for a Business Start-up allowance, described more fully later, in Chapter 5.

your abilities

You may have experience of the kind of business you intend to move into. However, if you intend to set up alone, not in partnership or as a franchise, there will be only you to attend to all of the different functions such as marketing, management, bookkeeping and planning. You will need to be energetic and organised.

Take a look at some of the characteristics needed to be successful in any business venture. Remember, though, that success is not certain, whether or not you have these qualities. Please tick either the 'Yes' or the 'No' box.

Are you sure that you are able to:

	Yes	No
Work unsocial hours	❏	❏
Work hard	❏	❏
Be persistent	❏	❏

Take frequent rejection ❏ ❏
Enthuse others ❏ ❏
Be decisive ❏ ❏
Be self-reliant ❏ ❏
Keep organised ❏ ❏
Stay motivated ❏ ❏
Sell against the odds ❏ ❏
Negotiate on all levels ❏ ❏

You should score 'Yes' at least eight times.

Do you have:

Clear personal objectives ❏ ❏
A high level of skill in your chosen field ❏ ❏
Open-mindedness, the ability to learn ❏ ❏
Self-discipline ❏ ❏
A strong will ❏ ❏
A friendly professional manner ❏ ❏

You should score 'Yes' at least five times.

This exercise may have given you thoughts that you did not have before. Again, it will be useful to summarise these.

Complete the following:

I believe I will succeed because _____

_____

_____

working from home: the family implications

For many would-be business people, one of the first hurdles to overcome is the cost of renting or buying premises from which to trade. However, the simple expedient of working from home, an increasingly popular option because of its cost-effectiveness, may be the best solution.

This option is far less expensive than buying or renting other premises, and you can be more flexible with regard to the hours you work. Since clients and customers very often never see the premises from which you do business, you need not be professionally compromised either. You save time and money by not having to travel to your workplace and, to some extent, your work can be combined with family life.

To create the right image, you will need to ensure that, during office hours at least, all telephone calls are channelled through you. Background noises that suggest you are operating from home should also be minimised.

Examples of the kind of work that can be conducted from home include:

- journalism;
- research;
- crafts;
- telesales;
- consultancy;
- teleworking;
- hypnotherapy;
- chiropody;
- photography;
- graphic design;
- teaching/coaching;
- hairdressing;
- catering;
- antique dealing;
- child minding;

- Web designing;
- artistic work;
- writing;
- brokerage;
- direct selling;
- driving instruction;
- some trades.

The most important thing to consider if you are working from home is: do you have the full cooperation and goodwill of your family? Working from home can provide more distractions than you might wish for, given the fact that you are trying to earn a living.

You need to make it clear to your family that this is your work, and it must be treated as such. They will need to agree in advance to respect the times you have set aside exclusively for your work. They will need to allow you to establish an office at home with all the proper facilities, in so far as you can afford them. They will need to keep interruptions to a minimum and protect you from the casual social caller.

You will need to be even more self-disciplined than you would be on 'proper' business premises. You should groom yourself each morning as if you were leaving the house to go to an outside place of work. This helps to avoid slipping into a sloppy attitude, and tones your mind for the rigours of the work routine.

By sticking to a strict routine with yourself and your family, and being seen to be doing so, your family and any visitors will gradually realise that this is 'a proper job' you are doing and begin to respect that. In the final analysis, people will take you at your own valuation.

action

- If you have a mortgage, check with the building society or bank to make certain there is no reason for them to object to the kind of business you will be running from home. If you are a tenant, read your lease and check with your landlord.

■ Keep your neighbours in mind, too. They are unlikely to object as long as the business does not intrude upon their lives by causing noise, parking problems, etc. People have an in-built contrariness, so you would do best to keep them informed of your intention rather than cause a complaint at a more crucial stage.

■ Check with your local authority, especially if you plan any alterations to your home – adding an extra room for an office or workshop, for example, for which you may need planning permission.

■ Get advice on whether or not you can claim tax relief against certain business expenses incurred from home. You may even be allowed to claim a proportion of your rent or mortgage against tax. But be careful. If you sell your house in the future, the Inland Revenue may wish to claim capital gains tax on some of the profit if you have made claims against tax for that part of the house which you use exclusively for business.

■ You may need to update your household insurance to cover working from home. Get in touch with your insurers.

■ If you will be using your car for the business, even travelling to and from sales appointments, it is best to inform your insurance company. This does not necessarily mean that your premium will be increased, but you do need to be thorough, in case there is ever a need to make a claim.

training and hard work

One source has it that while four out of five new businesses fail within the first five years, this ratio is reversed among those who have had some basic form of training in business prior to setting up. The *success* rate among this group is four out of five. Management training is particularly valuable.

Before you start your business, check with your local college for courses that might be able to give you the office skills you will need – bookkeeping or word processing, for example. There is usually a small fee for these classes; however, they train you while also providing a platform for you to meet the other 'students' who may be future customers, or may be in a business ready and able to offer useful advice.

Track down advice sources. New small firms that use relevant advice sources, such as enterprise agencies, are twice as likely to survive as new small firms in general. Enterprise agencies still exist in parts of the country, but many are now subsumed into Business Links. If you have Internet access, you'll find the National Federation of Enterprise Agencies (NFEA) at www.smallbusinessadvice.org.uk.

Among the most dangerous illusions of all is the illusion that results can be achieved easily. Fifty per cent of those who go into their own business work at weekends, one-third have taken only a short break in a year and one-fifth work 75 hours a week or more.

Are you well prepared? If you fail to prepare, you are preparing to fail.

'let's not overthink this, let's just do it'

You've given it constructive thought, considered the possible hitches, read the statistics and examined your conscience. You have decided you are the calibre of person needed to succeed in the venture you propose.

When a movie he is directing runs into a hitch, rather than enter into a rigmarole about it, Clint Eastwood is quoted as saying, 'Let's not overthink this, let's just do it.' At this stage, that's what you need to do. You have made the decision to do it, so what you need now is sensible advice on how to approach the practicalities of setting up your business. This you will get in the chapters that follow.

which business?

Which business should you be in? Roughly one in four of those who wish to start up their own business will not be sure which idea is best for them. A second category will find that close analysis shows their initial idea to be unsuitable.

In either of these instances, new ideas will be needed. Market research should pinpoint which kinds of small business are succeeding within the geographical area in which you will be trading. Would any of these suit you? If so, establish that there is room for you as another competitor, and be sure your talents can be adapted to the task. If not, seek training prior to starting up.

You may feel that your particular work experience determines the answer to this question, and that you should continue in the line of work you are used to. If your market research backs you up on this, your course is clear.

There are markets in which smallness seems to work well. Among these are bakeries, newsagents and sandwich bars, though entering into any of these businesses does not, of course, guarantee success.

buying an existing business

If you have the means to consider buying an existing business, be cautious and employ the services of the relevant experts to check it out. Buying a going concern may mean purchasing a package that includes premises, fixed assets, stock and goodwill.

Matters such as work in progress, the expertise needed to run the business and whether you will be taking on the company's debtors and creditors will need to be considered and carefully weighed.

You will also need to be assured in writing that the seller will not simply set up in competition to you nearby.

Have a shortlist of businesses to consider to keep your options open.

franchises

Franchises are a good means of drastically reducing the risk you take when setting out to become your own boss. One source has it that 95 per cent of franchisees remain in business. An established company will license you to sell its product or service in a designated area. You will benefit from its market position, the use of its procedures and products, help in setting up and corporate advertising. Certainly, you will have a far greater chance of staying the course because:

- You will be using a tried and tested formula that is working elsewhere for others.
- You will have the backing of an experienced organisation.
- Customers will already be aware of the brand name.

Franchising turns over £9.2 billion a year in the United Kingdom. You will know the more famous franchises that dominate most town centres: Swinton Insurance, Kall-Kwik, KFC, McDonald's, Prontaprint and Body Shop. The list is endless.

There are many lesser-known franchises that may suit your idea of being your own boss better. They will range from companies that unblock drains and mobile car valeting to sophisticated white-collar franchise opportunities in accountancy and main car dealerships. The choice for someone who is considering taking this route to being their own boss is bewildering and, as with all things, should be looked at with a cold professional eye.

Franchising is one business area where your experience does not have to be the basis for your choice. It will provide you with an opportunity to change tack from your previous career line, if that is what you wish. The reason is that good franchisors will train you to use their system, which will have been formulated so as to be easily digested by anyone with a modicum of business acumen.

In fact, as a rule of thumb, it is inadvisable to become involved in any franchise that seems unduly difficult to run.

That said, as with any situation in which you genuinely wish to be your own boss, you will have to be ready to work hard and invest a sizeable sum of your own money in the franchise. In the beginning in particular, the time and effort you will be asked to invest will be no less than in any other new business, despite the high level of support. It is this very support, bringing to you all there is to learn in this specialist area, that will demand a total commitment from you. The franchisor will not simply be looking for someone to invest funds, but will be carefully selecting an entrepreneur whose drive and product belief will help to ensure the continued success of their joint enterprise.

Although there are differing levels of investment, involvement, responsibility and returns, you will need to have capital available from savings, the cashing in of an investment, a legacy, redundancy money or a loan to invest in the franchise at your chosen level. The major clearing banks are likely to be more supportive of a franchise than of a brand-new unsupported idea.

If you have Internet access, there are various sites you will find useful, including uk.franchiseopportunities.com and www.british-franchise.org.uk. Otherwise, the *United Kingdom*

Franchise Directory is a good place to begin your research into franchises. This is published by Franchise Development Services Ltd, Franchise House, 56 Surrey Street, Norwich NR1 3DF (tel: 01603 620301). This address is also the base for the Franchise Advice Centre, and the *Franchise Magazine*.

Guide to Buying Your First Franchise (Kogan Page) explains what to look for and how to assess the right business for you, and includes a description of many current franchises. If you prefer real-time, one-to-one contact, you could attend one of the many events held throughout Britain each year. You'll find details of these on the British Franchise Association's Web site (address above), or contact your nearest Business Link.

When you are nearer to deciding which franchise you will be going for, have an accountant go over a copy of the relevant accounts and get the advice of a solicitor. The big banks have franchise units and are experienced at evaluating the financial viability of a proposal.

Make independent visits to some of the established franchisees and get their opinion of the franchise as an investment.

The questions you should ask your prospective franchisor should cover the following areas:

- What exactly will the support consist of? For example, site selection, launch, raising finance, marketing, central accounting, insurance?
- Will the training be continuous, and not just in the early days?
- What equipment will be included in the deal: computers, machinery, even uniforms?
- What rights does the contract entitle you to? For example, how big will your exclusive trading area be, will you be given all the necessary operating manuals, and so on?
- What are the exact short-, medium- and long-term costs that you will be expected to commit yourself to?
- What will be your share of the profit?

- What is the franchisor's business track record and how often is the product or service updated?
- What ratio of the franchisor's outlets continue to trade five years after opening?
- To what degree will the business be run by the franchisor, and what level of management input can you expect from them?

For literature on franchises call the British Franchise Association in Henley-on-Thames on 01491 578050.

direct selling

The Direct Selling Association, 29 Floral Street, London WC2F 9DP (tel: 020 7497 1234) has a list of member companies that are often looking for self-employed people to sell their products – usually direct to private homes. This is worth mentioning here because it is a simple route to setting up what will effectively be your own business. Alternatively, it could also prove a good second string to your bow. Training is often provided.

Though specific experience may not be required, all the other qualities you need to be successful in your own business are, not least determination. Products to be sold may include clothes, electrical appliances, reference books, toys, and so on. Sometimes distributors are required to pay for samples or catalogues.

The work can include the system known as party plan – calling on people's homes by appointment – and network marketing. Network marketing is based on the building up of a distribution network through your own contacts and their contacts, rippling out in wider and wider circles, thus increasing your potential market.

Direct selling is easier if you are naturally outgoing, and will not necessarily suit everyone – but it is a very flexible way of going it alone without a major financial commitment. It may suit those who are unable to raise finance in the usual way, and either run the operation in parallel with their own, or as a means of building up capital prior to changing tack.

researching your business idea

Effective marketing, tight financial controls and good forward planning will always underpin any successful enterprise. Market research and pricing should be done at this stage as part of your forward planning.

You may have heard of the four Ps of marketing. These are:

■ the *Product* or service you sell;
■ the *Price* you charge;
■ the *Place* from which your product or service is sold;
■ the *Promotion* and presentation of your product.

the product or service – is it right?

Even if you have decided what kind of business you intend to run, you will need to be sure there are sufficient customers out there to make it viable. You can help to establish this by market research.

To draw a military parallel, market research is to business what reconnaissance is to the armed forces. It is an attempt to know what lies ahead in order to deal with it properly.

The depth of research required depends on the kind of business you'll be entering. If you will be opening a new bakery, you'll need to be more thorough than if you were opening a market stall. The results of your research should indicate whether the business is a candidate for success or if you should look at other options.

The rule is that you should make what you can sell rather than sell what you can make. You may be able to make beautiful teddy bears, or you may be an excellent plasterer, but will enough people pay you to make enough teddies or plaster enough walls to be cost-effective?

Businesses selling goods should not rely on just one or two lines, but build up a list of items to further entice customers to buy. This is especially important if purchases are not repeated weekly, but are bought perhaps only once. Mail order selling in particular needs new items coming on stream in order to maintain customers' interest and obtain repeat custom.

This early stage is the best time to give consideration to the selection of goods you will be offering customers, as these will need to be costed out as part of the business plan.

Marketing is finding out what is needed by the customer and then supplying it at a profit. It is the opposite to expecting your product or service to be bought by the customer.

The methods of market research open to you are listed below.

1. desk research

- At home you can use telephone canvassing to speak to prospective customers, competitors and trade/business organisations.
- In the library, preferably the business or commercial section of your main library, you can refer to directories and market reports, the *Yellow Pages,* trade directories, local newspaper advertisements and the electoral register.
- There is a broad selection of useful sites to be found on the Internet, including a wealth of statistics and advice for new businesses. A good starting point is www.dti.gov.uk.

This kind of research will help you to establish who your competitors are, their size, how numerous they are, their turnover and where they choose to advertise.

If you are contemplating a mailshot, it will also provide you with contact names and addresses, either commercial or, in the case of the electoral register, domestic.

2. mobile research

Look at the local competition – what are their premises like? If they are a retailer, do they appear to have a good level of custom? Visit local industrial estates, business parks, chambers of commerce, trade organisations and business clubs.

3. street survey

If you will be selling to the public, arrange a set of relevant questions with yes/no answers. This could be choices of price, for example. You should ask about six questions or as many as comfortably take 30 seconds.

For the purpose of market research, 30 is the smallest number that can be safely taken as a sample representing everyone. However, with only 30 respondents, only a confidence level of 68 per cent can be assumed. Effectively, one-third of your sample will not be a good one.

You will need to know your target market:

- ■ Who are your prospective customers?
- ■ Are there enough of them?
- ■ Will they be buying on price or on quality?
- ■ Why will they buy?
- ■ Where are they situated and how many are there?
- ■ Where do they buy now?
- ■ Why should they change their supplier?
- ■ How wide is the area you will be able to take advantage of?

Usually, your trading will be done within a limited radius of about 30 kilometres, though the obvious exception would be trading via the Internet. You cannot reasonably expect to include prospective customers within a much wider band. If you live on the coast, however, much of the radius will be cut off, so you'll need to make up for that by radiating outward more on the precise area you have to serve.

Identify the competition:

■ Who are they?
■ Where are they?
■ Are they better or cheaper than you?
■ Are they growing in number, struggling or shrinking?
■ What are their strengths and weaknesses?
■ What size are they?
■ What is their turnover per annum?
■ What medium do they use to advertise?

Draw as accurate a picture of your potential market as you can. Do not let optimism cloud the realities. You need a clear and detailed image of your market and your place in it before you launch.

Ask yourself:

■ What is your competitive edge?
■ What differentiates you from the competition?
■ What can you offer that they don't?
■ How can you improve on what they are offering?
■ Is there a niche in the market as yet underserved?
■ Does the product or service have a repeat market?
■ Is the business subject to a demand cycle?

There is no need to be discouraged by competition. Its very existence is proof of a need for what you intend to offer. More seriously, if there is no competition, why not?

How you use the information you collate is more vital than the information itself.

You must:

■ Decide what you need to verify.
■ Structure the gathered facts coherently.
■ Look at the direction the research suggests.
■ Decide whether to stay on course, modify your direction or change.
■ Decide objectively.
■ Go forward with your decision.

That decision, based on the facts now available to you, may not be the one you started out with. It is unlikely that you need to be discouraged, but you may now choose to start more tentatively.

You could sample the realities of trading by taking the part-time option. This means that, should you have one, you keep your full-time job and carry on with your own business on evenings and weekends (but check whether your current contract of employment will let you do this). This is a particularly good idea with such things as arts and crafts, the cost of which, in an age of volume manufacturing, is always difficult to recoup.

If you do not have a full-time job, there is still room for choice. Perhaps your partner can continue working or take up new work? Or perhaps you can find a part-time job to help supplement the early days of your new venture? Of course, not every kind of business would fit into this regime.

Your market research data should be kept and updated and learnt from continuously.

To establish what difficulties may occur in the running of your business, visit a company that is trading but out of your area. As you will not be competing directly, they may well be happy to help. People like displaying their expertise.

If you felt it necessary, you could call under the guise of a customer. Come away with whatever literature, brochures and price lists you can.

Identify what will make your business different. You might open on Saturdays or Sundays; provide a wider choice; give a lifetime or money-back guarantee. You might offer something completely new, or simply put a new 'spin' on something old.

pricing

You will need to work out what you will charge for your product or service. Unless you are able to compete easily on being cheaper, don't. You are in business to make a profit, and that means earning enough to cover your personal and business outgoings, with some left over. It is easier to go down in price later if you must, but difficult to raise your prices without antagonising customers.

Estimated monthly business overheads include:

1. *fixed costs*, such as rent, insurance, depreciation;
2. *variable costs*: sales-related items such as travel, raw materials, plant hire, stationery.

The following will help you to estimate total monthly overheads. Modify the list to suit your circumstances.

Monthly overheads budget

	Per month £
Drawings	_____
Tax and National Insurance	_____
Rent and rates	_____
Loan repayments	_____
Bank charges	_____
Insurance	_____
Life assurance	_____
Electricity	_____
Phone	_____
Gas	_____
Water rates	_____
Transport	_____
Materials	_____
Plant hire	_____
Subcontracting	_____
Advertising	_____
Stationery	_____
Business cards	_____
Postage	_____
Subscriptions	_____

Office sundries   _____
Professional fees   _____
Depreciation   _____
Cleaning   _____
Contingency fund   _____

Overheads total   £ _____

To establish an hourly rate or a per item cost:

1. Carry forward monthly total outgoings from page 8.
2. Add monthly overheads total.
3. Add, say, 10 per cent of this new total as a profit.
4. Either divide total by number of working hours for hourly rate, or divide total by projected sales to get per item sales price.

Take into account that not all the hours you work will be productive – some will be spent prospecting, seeking and buying materials, some on administration. Therefore, if you expect to put in 40 hours per week, work out how many of those you can expect to use actually earning money.

Also, you must take out statutory holidays and your own annual holidays from the year's 52 weeks, leaving (say) 49 weeks. These three free weeks must still be paid for, though – bills won't go away.

Therefore, multiply (say) 30 hours per week by 49 weeks, which equals 1,470 productive hours per year. Divide this figure by 12 to give a monthly total, and use this as the figure you divide into the total sum you obtained by adding monthly outgoings with total overheads to give your hourly rate.

providing for illness or accident

Should you fall ill, and if you pay your Class 2 insurance stamps, as a self-employed person you can claim Incapacity Benefit. Note that the first three days from the date of your claim will not be included in your claim.

Your individual circumstances may affect the amount you can get, but the short-term lower rate (at the time of writing) is £53.50 per week. In addition to this, for each week that you provide a 'sick note' (Med 3 Certificate), you will be credited with a National Insurance contribution. If, however, you have claimed a small earnings exemption and do not pay your Class 2 contributions, you will not be eligible to claim this benefit.

You must also balance the cost of taking out some form of insurance to cover you while you are ill against the possibility of this happening. You can, for example, take out personal accident and sickness insurance, private medical insurance or permanent health assurance.

Pricing is a marketing, not an accounting, decision. The rule is that you should charge what the market will bear. If your price seems low, raise it. Market research will tell you if your price is competitive.

The pricing mechanism can be useful later to adjust demand, if this proves excessive. You raise your price until demand levels out. Your turnover might be less, but you have increased your profit margins.

Each product or service has its own *demand curve*. This is the line on a graph which relates sales volume to selling price, and which would show how sales volume is affected by any change in the selling price.

Your demand curve may be elastic: if you lower your price this might increase sales. In contrast, an inelastic demand curve means that, for whatever reason, your sales would not be favourably affected by lowering your price. In some cases, high prices are a perceived benefit as the product is made more exclusive. Who would expect a BMW to be cheap? Who would expect champagne to sell at £1 a bottle?

You must establish the optimum price that enables you to make a profit. You may not be able to establish this immediately, so err on the side of caution. Many believe that you should estimate what you need to charge and then double it.

If you price too highly, you won't sell. If you price to break even, you are not allowing for unforeseen expense, so you are undercharging. If you price too cheaply you will never be out of work, but you'll soon be out of business.

Once you have worked out your unit cost or hourly rate, check this against what is currently being paid in the marketplace. If the price is within the range currently being charged, good. Otherwise, re-examine your figures.

It cannot be repeated too often that you should avoid dropping your price. If you reduce your price, it will seem that you were trying to overcharge in the first place, and that will not earn you respect. You would do better to emphasise benefits. Price is only one consideration in a customer's lexicon. People often perceive better quality in a higher price. Value is more important.

Three points here are worth noting:

1. If your buyer is not the end-user, but is acting as a middleman or wholesaler, you need to have a price structure that will provide for the usual trade margin when your product is sold on.
2. Do not be surprised if the unit cost or hourly rate seems high compared to what you might expect as an employee.
3. Once you are trading, tell the customer the total price and break down all the benefits he or she gets by paying that. Your hourly rate might only serve to shock the lay person, who does not appreciate its components.

Buyer motivation is both:

1. *Surface;* for example:

   ■ need;
   ■ design;
   ■ performance;
   ■ packaging;
   ■ savings;
   ■ health benefits;
   ■ durability;
   ■ usefulness.

2. *Subliminal*; for example:

■ pride;
■ pleasure;
■ pressure;
■ fear;
■ envy;
■ approval;
■ sentiment
■ desire.

Pricing is a maze through which every business, new or old, must tread. Few will get it exactly right first time. The guideline is to sell up and negotiate down.

place

'Place' is where you put or place your product, or information about it, to ensure that it is easily seen, reached and bought by your customers. It means effective distribution to your chosen market.

If you will be working from home and selling a product, should you consider other points of distribution? Or an agent? Will the customer need to come to you, or will you offer immediate delivery?

You should see this part of the marketing strategy, as with all others, from the customer's point of view. How can you place what you are selling so that the customer needs to exert a minimum of effort to obtain or use it?

promotion

Promotion includes anything and everything that makes your company known and helps to move sales upwards.

In order to discover which form of promotion is best for your particular product or service, try each one when the time comes. You should find, however, that your market research shows what your competitors use, and this is likely to be the right one.

Forms of promotion and sources of publicity include:

- leaflets;
- canvassing;
- press editorial;
- mailshots;
- business cards;
- shop window advertisements;
- newspaper advertisements;
- trade magazine advertisements;
- *Yellow Pages* and *Thomson Directory*;
- vehicle signage;
- hoardings;
- posters;
- radio;
- television;
- phone box displays;
- exhibitions;
- taxi advertisements;
- directories;
- keyrings, badges or pens with your name and business details;
- word of mouth;
- the Internet.

Word of mouth is not enough by itself to secure your livelihood, but this kind of referral is the best form of advertisement for your company once it is up and running. People trust the judgement of someone they know.

If you offer a specialist product or service, then you probably need to use a trade or business journal directed at your segment of the market. Usually, though, for smaller firms just starting up, the local paper proves the most cost-effective because:

1. It is not a long-term commitment like directories are, and as such only requires a minimal outlay.
2. The advertisement can be withdrawn, reduced or changed at short notice.

Someone once said that half of advertising is wasted – the problem is knowing which half. I would disagree, because market research will soon show you which means of promotion is best for your product or service.

When you are in business, every caller should be asked where he or she heard of you, and the answers recorded. A regular review of these answers will soon show where the money is well used and where it is wasted.

An enquiry alone is not enough to justify spending more money on a particular form of promotion, though: that enquiry must turn into a sale. It is the actual sales that each source generates that will show you where your money is best spent.

Once you have discovered the best means of promotion for your enterprise, you might try a mix of the others to lift your profile in the area as part of the initial launch.

Telephone canvassing can be a very effective way to secure appointments for any business. The techniques required for this are looked at in Chapter 8. We shall look at mailshots as well, which can be combined with telephone selling very effectively.

This chapter has touched upon only part of the marketing function – an essential part at this stage of your affairs. Marketing and selling are looked at more fully in Chapter 8.

professional advice

Good advice before starting up your own business can double your chances of success. Advice from experienced business-people, accountants, solicitors and bank managers should be obtained not only at the outset, but continuously. The initial consultation is often free, so ask about this when making an appointment. Have a list of matters to discuss, so you get the best value from each interview.

The purpose behind taking advice is to ensure, so far as possible, that each decision you take is an informed one. It should prove an enjoyable learning experience and your confidence will grow with your knowledge.

In matters of law, taxation or regulations of any sort, expert knowledge can be taken as read. However, it is sensible to obtain more than one opinion where an element of judgement is required – where a loan is involved, for example.

Though seeking advice may seem time-consuming, you will be more than repaid in the future when your time will be at a premium. Pocket your pride, listen and learn.

The most obvious source of help might be someone you know who is already experienced in business. If you need advice from a professional of any sort, ask your acquaintances for contacts. This has the advantage of putting the relationship with the professional on a more intimate footing immediately.

If you prefer, you can let your fingers do the walking and turn to the *Yellow Pages* or *Thomson Directory*, checking the relevant section for a solicitor, an accountant or a nearby bank, depending on what you require.

There is no need to feel at all obliged to stay with the first adviser you meet. As in all interpersonal relationships, a great deal of how you feel about the advice you get is down to compatibility. If you are not happy, try someone else.

Free sources of information and training will include the small business adviser at your local bank. You may be well advised to make appointments with more than one bank, so as to be able to decide which, if any, might be of most use. Their advice may not be wholly disinterested.

government help for new businesses

Small Business Service and Business Link

The Small Business Service (SBS), part of the Department of Trade and Industry (DTI), provides links to other relevant organisations and operates a number of schemes and initiatives to help small businesses. From this source you can access information on the Business Start-up Programme, on how to obtain finance, on how to make use of expertise that is available to you as a start-up, on how to improve business-to-business transactions and on how to measure and improve efficiency.

The SBS manages the national Business Link service throughout England, which provides independent, impartial advice to help new start-ups or those about to set up in business, as well as small to medium-sized enterprises (SMEs) generally. The SBS can provide you with information on such resources as the national Phoenix Fund, which helps to encourage entrepreneurship in disadvantaged areas, and the

SBS Business Incubation Fund, which aims to improve the chances of survival and growth of start-up and early-stage business. Or you can ask about the SBS Smart Grant, which is designed to help individuals and SMEs to make better use of technology and to develop technologically innovative products and processes.

In partnership with others, the SBS has also developed the Farm Business Advice Service, which can provide up to three days of personalised business advice to develop an action-plan for progress.

The DTI's enquiry line is 020 7215 5000 and their Web address is www.dti.gov.uk.

At any one time there are hundreds of different schemes in operation, constantly changing, lapsing or being cancelled or renewed. That these are run by scores of different 'awarding bodies' means that you'll need great determination and patience to work through the maze alone. All the more reason, then, to take advice beforehand.

The first point of contact (for England) should be Business Link, whose central phone line number (at local call rates) is 0845 600 9006, or through the Web on www.businesslink.org. In other parts of the United Kingdom advice and services akin to that offered by Business Links in England are to be found from such organisations as:

■ Small Business Gateways (SBGs) in Lowland Scotland (tel: 0845 609 6611);
■ Business Information Sources (BISs) in Highland Scotland (tel: 01463 234 171);
■ the Welsh Development Agency (tel: 0845 777 5577};
■ InvestNI in Northern Ireland (tel: 028 9049 0486).

All of the above are initial points of contact and will point you towards your nearest local provider if they themselves do not fulfil your requirements. They can also be contacted by way of the Business Link Web site, address above.

If you need access to a Web site, many local libraries offer an Internet service free of charge, though you will need to book your slot. Most Web sites will have useful links to other similar sites, thus proving doubly effective in helping you to uncover the exact information you require.

Often, assistance for start-up enterprises is:

- ■ sector specific; that is, aimed at, say, new companies involved in technology or the arts;
- ■ area specific; that is, one area may receive both European and central government funding whereas another may not.

A visit to your Jobcentre is often worthwhile in helping to sift through exactly what training and advice you can access where you are. There you should find a good cross-section of leaflets aimed at those who intend to start their own business or, to put it another way, become self-employed.

There are companies that, in association with government agencies such as Jobcentre Plus and Business Link, provide support services to start-ups across the board. Consult an adviser at your Jobcentre who will help you establish who these might be. Taking advice and training prior to start-up will, according to DTI figures, increase your business's chance of survival by as much as 20 per cent.

Local Enterprise Agencies

There are also 180 Local Enterprise Agencies (LEAs), usually staffed by local people who are already in business and can give advice tailored to local conditions.

LEAs are supported by a combination of local businesses, banks and local authorities. Their purpose is to offer independent, confidential counselling to businesspeople about to start or already started.

As well as general counselling, there will be specialist counselling available from experts in varying aspects of business. Their proficiency will cover marketing, exporting, property, finance, the single European market, business planning, accounting, tax and insurance and manufacturing. For the address of your local enterprise agency, call the National Federation of Enterprise Agencies on 01234 354055 or access their Web site, www.nfea.com, and www.smallbusinessadvice.org.uk.

help for younger entrepreneurs
the Prince's Youth Business Trust

If you are aged between 18 and 30, the Prince's Youth Business Trust can offer business advice, marketing opportunities and, possibly, financial assistance. The financial side will be looked at in Chapter 5, Raising Finance.

The Prince's Youth Business Trust is at 18 Park Square East, London NW1 4LH (tel: 020 75433 1234). The Web address is www.princes-trust.org.uk.

Livewire

Funded by Shell, Livewire offers help and advice to people aged between 16 and 30 who wish to become self-employed. Cash awards are made to eligible applicants. The initial contact is through Livewire, Freepost, Newcastle upon Tyne NE1 1BR. The Livewire Hotline is 0845 7573252. The Web address is www.shell-livewire.org.

trade associations
chambers of commerce

Your local chamber of commerce can offer such facilities as the use of a conference room, and lists of local businesses, if you choose to pay the subscription and join. It will give you the opportunity to meet other businesspeople, and such contacts can be very rewarding.

Some more progressive chambers may offer day nurseries, seminar programmes, consultancy and training initiatives. You will also have access, through the local branch, to a full range of services offered by the main chambers.

the Federation of Small Businesses

The Federation of Small Businesses, Sir Frank Whittle Way, Blackpool Business Park, Blackpool, Lancashire FY4 2FE (tel: 01253 336000; Web site www.fsb.org.uk), is a campaigning and pressure group for the self-employed and small businesses generally.

Benefits of membership include a legal fees and insurance scheme; a 24-hour legal advice service to members on business or private matters; advice on tax and dealing with the Department of Social Security, value added tax, safety at work, etc. The Federation also offers favourable health insurance rates for members and their families, and a debt collection service. Joining fees are on a rising scale.

The Federation is non-profit making and not politically affiliated. It is the largest of its sort and lobbies Parliament on behalf of the interests of small businesses.

the Forum of Private Business

The Forum of Private Business, Ruskin Chambers, Drury Lane, Knutsford, Cheshire WA16 6HA (tel: 01565 634467; Web site www.fpb.co.uk) is a non-profit seeking, non-partisan lobby group dedicated to promoting free enterprise. It was formed in 1977 with the aim of giving private business owners a real say in any legislation affecting their profitability.

It was lobbying of Parliament by the FPB that brought about the phasing in of the Uniform Business Rate over five years, pre-notification of charges by the banks and removal of most small firms from the inheritance tax net.

The organisation provides instructive booklets which it refers to as 'profit builders' and which help its members to negotiate reductions in bank charges, get bills paid faster and prepare contracts of employment. It also provides an information service to help small business owners make correct decisions on the more than 3,000 issues that would normally be encountered in any business year.

business clubs

Local small business clubs are very useful to join at the beginning, as you will meet people in the same situation as yourself. Such contacts may enable you to find the necessary support to your morale that many more objective organisations cannot offer. They also usually enable you to find an outlet for your particular business, in that members of your club will use your business before they will use a stranger's.

Usually the club will hold regular meetings, activities and presentations with a broad subject base to appeal to all businesses of all sizes. The advice given at presentations will be useful, as will the advice given by those in the club who may have more experience than you. The advantage of seeking advice prior to setting up in business is that you can learn from other people's mistakes, perhaps avoiding them yourself.

other sources of information
local libraries

Check with your main central library to see if they have a small business information unit. Those that exist are there to help small firms negotiate the information maze, and are often staffed by people whose advice is based on business experience. This service is usually free if you are within the catchment area of the library.

The unit can also be used as a credit reference agency and, using the library's vast resources, will be able to point you towards specialist technical information. Many can also provide mailing lists on either hard copy or floppy disk along with address labels if required. There will be a charge for this service. As already mentioned, many local libraries offer free Internet access.

teleworking

Membership of the Telework Association (TCA), established in 1993, is open to any individual or organisation whose work is carried out mainly at a distance from its source. This usually means through the use of computers and telecommunication.

Relevant employment could include technical writing, software support, accountancy, public relations, data processing, research, journalism and sales.

The advantages of joining include access to relevant publications and training courses. You will also be a member of a national network of contacts, which should prove advantageous to the imaginative.

Members receive *The Teleworking Handbook* as part of their fee, and TCA also publish a bi-monthly magazine called *Teleworkers*. They can be contacted at TCA, Freepost, CV2312, WREN, Kenilworth, Warwickshire CV8 (tel: 0800 616008; Web site www.telework.org.uk).

Other useful Web sites under this heading include www.homeworking.com or the BT working from home Web site at www.wfh.co.uk. If you've got time on your hands, and Internet access, type keywords such as 'start-up UK' into a search engine and you'll be presented with a wealth of useful links. Publications such as the *Which? Guide to Working from Home* by Lynn Brittney or the monthly magazine *Making Money* are also useful.

As should always be the case, research companies and offers as thoroughly as possible before deciding what to go for.

questions to ask advisers

■ How will self-assessment affect me as a start-up?
■ Is there any grant I can apply for?
■ How do I raise finance?
■ Do I need to register for VAT?
■ Who can help me to prepare/check my business plan?
■ Should I do my own accounts?
■ What further training do I need?
■ Where can I get it?
■ Should I be a sole trader, a limited company or a part-nership? (These are explained in Chapter 6.)
■ What other suggestions do you have to help me ensure I'm as prepared as possible before I start up?

Bring a list of questions such as this to each appointment with an adviser. Take note of their replies. Listen carefully.

the business plan

purpose of the business plan

You have assessed yourself and the business you are going to start up and taken appropriate advice. Now all this effort must be put to practical use in the business plan.

The business plan provides a good basis upon which to negotiate finance, if this is required. It also acts as a step-by-step explanation of how you intend to achieve your business success.

In it you will be looking at methods to turn your business idea into a reality. You will be making the results of your efforts so far into a formal and factual document.

Apparently, fewer than two-thirds of businesses prepare plans before starting up. According to research by Shell Livewire, those with regularly updated business plans had an average profit margin of 54 per cent, compared to only 35 per cent for those that did not. Interestingly, 43 per cent of 'grey' start-ups (businesses started by people aged over 50) prepare a business plan, compared to only 23 per cent of those started by younger people.

format of the business plan

There is no standard format to which you must adhere. However, the plan should convince any interested party, including yourself:

- that you are capable in your field;
- that you have done the necessary groundwork;
- that you have a realistic view of what is to come and where you are going;
- that you know how to get there.

Begin by looking at the business plan as a business project. Start as you mean to go on, by producing a solid, professional document. It should be typed, not handwritten. You should have at least two copies, one for safekeeping, and one to post to prospective lenders prior to an arranged meeting.

When the plan is completed to your satisfaction, it should be looked over for approval by a business adviser or an accountant prior to being presented in its final form.

The major banks, along with their other start-up literature, have free booklets on business planning which will be given to you on request. Obviously, any submission to a bank must be in their required form.

The length of the final document will vary. It could number 3 pages or 40. Keep it clear and take the time required to do it well. The person who will be reading your business plan will not necessarily understand your business sector. You should give precise details.

In the business plan, you will be:

- saying what you are going to say;
- saying it;
- saying that you've said it.

Some or all of the following must be considered for inclusion in the plan, depending on the nature of your business:

1. An introduction

    - This is where you grab the attention of the reader.
    - Give an overview.
    - Keep it brief.
    - Use short sentences.
    - Use shorter words where possible.

The introduction should describe the experience and strengths you have, providing a suitably tailored CV that demonstrates your ability to run the proposed business.

Any partners or members of your team will need to be similarly described.

2. The product or service

■ What is it?
■ What are your reasons for believing that it will sell?
■ To whom and to how many will you be selling it?
■ Is there room for your business in its market sector?
■ What is your position within that sector?
■ How does your past experience tie in?
■ If it doesn't, what steps have you taken to rectify this?
■ What premises will you need, if not operating from home?

3. The marketing strategy

■ What are your main business goals?
■ What are your other goals?
■ What steps will you be taking to achieve these?
■ What outside influences will affect your business?
■ What inside influences will affect your business?

At this point you might use what is known as the PEST and the SWOT formula. PEST deals with outside influences. The acronym comes from:

■ Political;
■ Economic;
■ Social;
■ Technological.

For example:

■ Is there a change of government imminent which may affect the rate at which VAT is charged?
■ Does the fact that the economy is in recession (say) favour your business (because there are lower wages, maybe)?

■ Does the fact that there are more single parents than ever before affect you? (Maybe you'll be offering a nursery facility.)

■ Does the rate of technological change affect your ability to compete in any way? (Can you afford the latest equipment?)

SWOT deals with influences *inside* your proposed business:

■ Strengths;
■ Weaknesses;
■ Opportunities;
■ Threats.

For example, you may be one of only a few thatchers in your part of the country, which should put you in a strong position given that the custom is there. But can you sell well? Is this a weakness? You may believe that the fact that a local thatching firm has just closed is an opportunity for you to step into the vacant space. The threat may come from others who have come to the same conclusion at the same time.

4. Budgets and forecasts

■ an overhead budget;
■ a profit and loss account;
■ a cash flow forecast.

an example of a business plan

To help you construct your own business plan, it is probably instructive to include an example here.

This is a real business plan that was used to obtain an overdraft facility. The details of market research were correct at the time the plan was used.

PRECISION MARKETING

'SENSIBLE SALESMANSHIP FOR SMALL BUSINESSES'

BUSINESS PLAN

4 December 1986

---

1. introduction

It seems reasonable to say that small firms must think in terms of small sums, carefully spent to the best advantage. The service PRECISION MARKETING will offer is likely to pay for itself and earn more on top for the end-user.

1.1 personal history
Started with the Institute of Bankers in London before moving on to work for a mortgage broking firm in sales. Next joined a London and Lagos computer systems house, serving on the sales management committee.

After a brief period teaching English abroad, moved to the north-west of England and helped set up a family firm, acting as new business manager and generating 41 per cent of all new leads by means of direct mail. This company now turns over £330,000 per annum.

Realised there is a need for a direct mail service for small businesses.

2. the service

Trading as PRECISION MARKETING, the new company will generate business leads on behalf of customers. Direct mail will be used as a medium to achieve this, an especially tailored sales letter being written in each case.

After consultation with the customer, a section of his market will be targeted, a list prepared or purchased, the agreed number of mailshots printed and all labelling, folding, inserting, sealing, franking and mailing undertaken as part of the package.

PRECISION MARKETING will also offer a telephone-sales follow-up facility.

2.1 location
The business will be run from home in an office separate from the house itself. This will be less costly than an office elsewhere. The time that would otherwise be spent travelling to a more distant workplace can be used more positively. Business will be conducted within a 20-mile radius of these premises.

2.2 medium-term
In the second year, PRECISION MARKETING expects to employ a tele-sales person on five afternoons. The afternoons are stipulated because of the cheaper call rates then.

This will free time to concentrate on a greater number of customers, thus increasing turnover.

It is intended that local advertising agencies will be approached at this stage with a view to PRECISION MARKETING being subcontracted to them.

3. the market
3.1 the target market

Those who could make best use of PRECISION MARKETING are small firms that are selling to business (as opposed to households).

It is often the case that the proprietor of a small firm is an expert at what he does, but not an expert at marketing his product or service.

Those under the auspices of the Enterprise Allowance Scheme may be a case in point. I have obtained a list of 200 such firms from the Merseyside Development Corporation.

3.2 market research conducted
From Post Office figures:

- 81 per cent of business people generally read direct mail.
- 60 per cent generally find it interesting.
- 77 per cent would rather receive it than not.
- 94 per cent like receiving it when it is relevant to them.

The Post Office's predicted response rate to direct mail can be quadrupled by:

- printing not just the target company's name on the envelope, but a contact name too;
- following up the mailing by telephone shortly afterwards.

Volume growth of advertising per media 1975–1982 (Source: Advertising Association):

Press	−5.3 per cent
Television	+5.0 per cent
Direct mail, general	−104 per cent
Direct mail, business & industrial	+24 per cent

Clearly, direct mail is a growth industry. More than that, it is still very much under-exploited, as witnessed by this excerpt from the international section of the American magazine *Direct Marketing, February 1986 edition:*

> Although in the UK some 50 per cent of the top 100 companies planned to use direct mail, this compares with 89 per cent in Switzerland (for example). There is scope for development, especially among small firms.

This was further borne out by research that we conducted at the Merseyside Development Corporation's South Dock Estate Enterprise Workshops. Businesses were interviewed in person and 50 per cent of these expressed interest in the service that PRECISION MARKETING intends to offer.

One company actually wanted us to start immediately.

3.3 proposed selling methods

Cold calling in person has the advantage of being able to assess the firm you will be dealing with more easily, and vice versa.

Whereas larger firms require a more formal approach, very small firms such as those already visited during market research seem to respond better to cold calling than tele-sales.

It is likely that a mixture of both methods will be used.

3.4 sales forecast

Presently, over a 48-week first year (allowing for Christmas, Easter, bank holidays and vacation) a projected average of 1.5 projects per week will produce a small trading profit.

The logistics of winning the projects to begin with must be allowed for, and must be continuous, so a six-day week is likely.

In order to achieve the necessary increase in productivity during PRECISION MARKETING's second year, it is anticipated that a part-time employee will be enrolled.

There will be a repeat market and, ultimately, much of the business's income will derive from a database of established customers.

3.5 competition

The nub of the business will be copywriting, though a more general classification would be direct response marketing. Thus, research has concentrated upon the preponderance, or otherwise, of copywriters, and, as an extension of that, the kind of organisation for which they might work.

The clearest implication of this research is that copywriters are usually employed as outworkers, and so act in a freelance capacity.

The *European Direct Mail Data Book* lists 103 British and European mailing houses, 17 consultancies and 23 advertising agencies that offer specialist services to direct mail users.

Of the 17 consultancies to which PRECISION MARKET-ING can be compared, not one had more than 19 employees, and many had only one. Turnover started at £50,000 per annum.

It was standard to expect payment in advance, and in most cases, minimum-value orders were specified.

The nearest registered consultant is in Batley, West Yorkshire.

Of the 23 advertising agencies offering services to direct mail users, none were near Liverpool or Southport, the towns where the bulk of PRECISION MARKETING customers must be found. Most of these agencies were in the London area.

Advertising agencies in Southport offer a leaflet design and artwork facility, but no full-time copywriter, in so far as reference books and discreet telephone enquiries can ascertain.

Also, advertising agencies usually promote themselves through specialist magazines, but do not actively seek business in the way that PRECISION MARKETING will be doing.

Mailing houses such as Focus and Vernons can be found in small numbers in Liverpool, but their bias is towards the householder: ie mail order.

Some freelancers advertise in the broadsheet newspapers. I have obtained literature from these. One is a housewife in Peterborough, another an ex-businessman in Halifax, and a third, the busiest, a businesswoman operating from Bournemouth. All are happy to contract nationwide. PRECISION MARKETING's fees will be pitched competitively, taking into account what information is to hand. The service will offer the advantage of being on the spot, rather than remote as in the cases quoted.

3.6 reasons for confidence
Reasons for confidence include:

- experience of selling on all levels;
- experience of direct mail campaigns;
- experience of starting and working with small businesses.

The shortest distance between two points (the vendor and the buyer) is a straight line. There is no more direct route than direct mail, with the exception of the telephone.

Direct mail is effective marketing offering profitable results for each investor. It is a goal-directed and precise science. It is proactive and positive.

It is possible to know almost to the last penny what value is obtained from each advertising pound. With most other media, this is not always the case.

Direct mail can be used in advertising, direct selling, generating sales leads, product testing, public relations, image building and market research.

It is cost-effective and can be monitored and controlled at almost all stages. It is a growth industry that is growing because of its proven merit. (As a matter of interest, London Bridge was sold by direct mail.)

It is a device well suited for use by any cost-conscious business manager.

Personal experience has proved that up to 41 per cent of all business turnover can be successfully generated by the proactive use of this excellent medium.

4. budgets and forecasts

Please find attached:

- ■ an overheads budget;
- ■ a profit and loss account;
- ■ a cash flow forecast.

Here the main body of the business plan ends, and we turn our attention to item 4 above (Budgets and forecasts).

overheads budget

You have already seen an example of a monthly overheads budget in Chapter 2. It will not be difficult to extend that budget to encompass business outgoings over a year. You might need to add entertaining expenses, or extra salaries for staff if these are relevant, plus whatever else is relevant to your own business.

Usually, you will also need to show a projection for at least Year 2 – and Year 3 in many cases.

So your new budget should be structured in the following manner:

Overheads Budget

	Year 1	Year 2	Year 3
Drawings			
Rent and rates			
Electricity			
Phone			
Transport			
Advertising			
Insurance			
Assurance			
Stationery			
Business cards			
Postage			
Subscriptions			
Office sundries			
Professional fees			
Loan repayments			
Bank charges			
Depreciation			
Materials			
Plant hire			
Subcontracting			
Cleaning			
Salaries			
Entertaining expenses			
Contingency fund			
Overhead totals			

You should already know your hourly rate or per item cost, as calculated in Chapter 2. For the projected profit and loss account you will need to estimate your sales turnover for the period in question.

Unless you have already got advance orders for your 'product' – and here the word means either your service, your manufactured item or whatever it is you intend to offer – it will be difficult to be certain of the quantity you will sell. You are better to err on the side of caution and expect there to be a fallow period at the start, while you build up custom.

If, for example, you are repairing washing machines on site, it should be possible to charge an hourly rate, added to a call-out rate, perhaps. In other instances, though, charging an hourly rate could mean that you are operating at a loss. It may be advisable to specify minimum-value orders.

For example, if you are a plasterer and have invested in tools, scaffolding, trestles, scaffold planks, a storage shed, a cement mixer and so on, it would not be realistic for you to charge for less than a full day. By the time you have loaded up, been to the builder's yard for materials, unloaded, set up your scaffolding, made the first mix, prepared the area to be plastered, covered up the driveway and windows, and protected the next-door neighbour's driveway too, a half-day may have elapsed and not one trowel of mortar will have been laid on the wall. You will then have to do much of what you have done already in reverse, unless the scaffolding is required in the same place the following day. Consequently, you may only have spent three hours in front of the wall actually plastering, but the job will have taken a full day.

It will be up to you to demonstrate to your customer why the patch of perished plaster outside his upstairs window will mean his paying for a day of your time. Alternatively, you could turn the job down rather than make a loss. Unless you are subcontracting to a builder, in which case there may be a pattern to your work, you will find that domestic customers usually like you to start quickly. Taking a loss-making job might mean having to turn down a profitable job in the next breath. So don't waste your time. It is natural to feel a sense of panic, and to take anything that is offered, but you have to stick to your guns and aim to make a profit – which is the purpose of being in business.

sales turnover

The sales turnover is the hinge upon which all else turns. From it you will decide whether you need larger premises than an office or workshop at home can provide. From it, too, you will be able to ascertain the level of investment your business will require, how large a loan if any is needed, what machinery/office equipment you should purchase, whether you'll need to employ others, and so on.

Your estimate of sales turnover can be modified regularly once you actually begin, and this will in turn affect your entire projection. The best guideline is to dampen your optimism at this point. Most new businesses tend to paint too glowing a picture.

In the case of the washing machine repairer mentioned, payment will be on completion of each job. This will usually be the case with the plasterer too. If your business does not allow this, you will need to take into account the time lag between completion of the work and the actual date you expect payment. This can be considerable and can make the difference between staying in business or failing. Banks tend to be interested in 'real' money, not invoices that may or may not be paid.

profit and loss account

The profit and loss account for the business plan should be broken down into months. The first month's figures in your case will be the actual month you begin trading – not necessarily January. For this reason, the example that follows will use numbers 1 to 12 to represent the months in the trading year.

Again, you will need to subtract from or add to the profit and loss account to suit your particular circumstances. If you get any allowances or financial support from sources such as the Prince's Trust, then this, obviously, will be shown as 'money in'. If the support comes in the form of a grant, you could spread this over 12 months to help meet the cost of living.

The monthly overheads figure is now obtained by dividing your Year 1 overheads total by 12. The depreciation, on machinery or plant, is likewise broken down.

Your personal drawings will be your income from the business, and this should be enough to cover your own outgoings as established under your review of your personal finances in Chapter 1.

The interest on the amount you intend to borrow, if applicable, will be easily worked out from tables, which a lender will be happy to supply you with in advance. This is also the case with bank charges, though there may be cheaper charges for new businesses if your bank has special deals for new businesses.

The 'Total out' will be subtracted from the 'Total in' and this will give a pre-tax, bottom-line total for each month. In the early months, this may be a loss. This exercise will enable you to estimate when you expect to break even.

For some of us that might take two years. This is not necessarily anything to be overly concerned about, as long as that was foreseen in the projections, and it is expected to go into profit afterwards.

An important part of the function of any business plan is to anticipate troughs and peaks in advance so appropriate financial arrangements can be put in place.

Projected profit and loss account

Month	1 2 3 4 5 6 7 8 9 10 11 12 Total
Prince's Trust	
Sales	
Total in	
Overheads	
Drawings	
Materials	
Depreciation	
Interest	
Bank charges	
Total out	
Pre-tax profit or loss	

Years 2 and 3 can be detailed on separate sheets.

cash flow forecast

Now we move on to the cash flow forecast. It is often thought that new businesses that fail can be classified under two main headings:

■ those that do not sell enough of their product;
■ those that sell too much of their product.

This may appear contradictory at first. The first possibility is probably clear to us all, but the second may need explanation.

When a company over-sells (also known as 'over-trading'), it often has too much of its capital tied up in stock to cater for the demand it has generated. Since payment for each sale may be delayed for up to three months, the company's supply of real cash dries up. Ironically, though technically profitable, it cannot pay its day-to-day bills, and so may be forced by its creditors to close down.

Chapter 8 shows you ways to help ensure that you sell enough of your product.

As for over-trading, the cash flow forecast is designed to show in advance where there will be shortfalls. This means that you can adjust your plans to try to avoid this happening. Or, if you intend to arrange an overdraft facility, you can inform your lender of the months when you expect to need the overdraft.

Your monthly sales turnover is carried forward from the last exercise. The actual payments from customers in each month will not necessarily mirror this figure, depending on credit arrangements agreed.

The net cash flow is the difference between the total money in and the total money out. Remember, these balances may not always be positive.

The opening balance for each month is the previous month's closing balance carried forward. This is added to the net cash flow of that month to give the new closing balance.

The closing balance in each month's column represents cash available at that time. The months are numbered 1 to 12 as in the profit and loss account.

Cash flow forecast

Month	1 2 3 4 5 6 7 8 9 10 11 12 Total
Sales	
Customer payments	
Prince's Trust	
Other business income	
Total	
Materials	
Salaries	
Drawings	
Rent	

Rates
Office expenses
Insurance
Other
Capital expenditure

Total

_____

Net cash flow

Opening balance

Closing balance

Not only should you prepare a cash flow forecast for the year ahead, but you should prepare a smaller cash flow forecast each month for the next quarter-year. This may be kept simple, and added to as required. You may find the exercise awkward at first, but will soon be doing it with ease.

You have to be sure that you will have sufficient funds on hand to keep the business's day-to-day expenses paid, or to have arranged or increased an overdraft limit to cover the troughs that the forecast will allow you to anticipate.

An example of a simple forecast follows:

Monthly cash flow forecast

	Month 1 £	Month 2 £	Month 3 £
Income			
Cash from sales	350	525	600
Prince's Trust	320	320	320
Other receipts, (such as capital introduced)	1,000		
Total expected in	1,670	845	920
Outgoings			
Materials	85	105	150

Drawings	600	600	600
Office expenses	11	25	25
Capital expenditure	700	150	–
Insurance	65	65	65
Petrol	20	20	20
Road tax	65	–	–
Advertising	150	100	75
Sundry overheads	35	35	35
Total expected out	1,731	1,100	980
Net cash flow (brackets mean deficit)	(61)	(255)	(60)
Opening balance (brought forward)	–	(61)	(316)
Closing balance (carried forward)	(61)	(316)	(376)

Looking at the cash flow forecast above makes it clear that action needs to be taken to either reduce, clear or cater for the negative balances. This could be done by increasing sales, reducing costs or arranging an overdraft of £400. This doesn't have to be used, but will act as a buffer or safety net.

As you see, this predicted monthly cash flow forecast is a useful business device, and should act as a motivator for you.

Note that the figures shown are purely notional and entirely for the purpose of the exercise.

bad debt provision

Depending on the business you are in, bad debt provision is likely to prove a not easily quantifiable cost. It makes good sense to build up a fund to protect yourself against this unfortunate aspect of being in business.

There are specialist insurance companies that offer policies to help cater for bad debts. These are called Credit Insurance

Policies but are technically bad debt protection. However, they are only available for businesses dealing with businesses and are prohibitively priced. Contact your local broker for advice.

In the following chapter we look at raising finance, which is where the business plan comes into play.

raising finance

For a small business to become established, grow and increase its productivity and efficiency, it is essential that it has access to sufficient financial backing.

Looking at your business plan will help you to decide how much, if anything, you need to borrow for starting capital.

The business plan will also help to establish how much you will need for working capital. This is the amount you require to cover troughs in trading and any costs necessary to keep your business viable. Later you will need capital for expansion and growth, but this chapter is mainly concerned with raising start-up and working capital.

It could be said that there are three ways of obtaining outside money to use in your business: you can borrow it, get a grant, or get someone to invest in your business for a return on that investment. This last is called equity or risk capital.

Even if, for your own reasons, you limit this exercise to (say) the banks, the golden rule is *shop around*. Not only might you get better terms by shopping around, but you are more likely to find an individual with whom you are happy to do business. (Access to the Internet makes this task less onerous than it once was.) This preparation will matter greatly at a later stage in your business when the unforeseen occurs and you have need of a sympathetic and flexible approach from your financial adviser.

Interest rates charged should be seen in terms of how far away they are from the bank base rate.

You should seek objective advice from some of the sources referred to in Chapter 3 about which lenders can offer you the best deal, taking all factors into account.

At this stage you must decide to ask for too much rather than too little. If you borrow too little, because you've under-estimated how much you need or because you feel an element of timidity, you are building in a potential cash flow shortage. This could mean being unable to meet demand because of insufficient funds to buy raw material, for example. That in turn could mean dissatisfied customers and lost trade. It will also mean that your judgement will be called into question when you have to admit to the lender that all your careful planning did not enable you to cater for this outcome.

One theory has it that you should estimate what you need to borrow and then double it, such is a new business's propen-sity to underestimate the capital needed. On the other hand, you must use your judgement to ensure that you do not run the risk of over-exposing your business.

Sources of borrowing could include yourself, your business partner(s), your spouse or partner, your parents, your friends, the bank, finance companies, building societies, ven-ture capitalists, government or European Union schemes and the Prince's Youth Business Trust. One source you will sel-dom see mentioned is a credit union. Let us look at each of these separately.

yourself

In most cases a lender will ask how much of your own funds you will be investing in your business and this will then be cal-culated as a proportion of the entire amount required. You will be expected to show faith by committing to between one-third and one-half of the total amount in question.

If you have your own capital in sufficient amounts to start the business without external funding, should you use it alone? Shouldn't you spread the risk?

your business partners

We will be looking at the advantages and disadvantages of having a partner or partners in your enterprise in Chapter 6. At this stage, however, the relevant questions to ask yourself are how will any investments made by your partner(s) influence the balance of power within the company? How will their investment, if it is greater than yours, influence the shared decision-making?

your spouse or life partner

If your spouse or life partner is not a partner in the firm, then perhaps this option for finance deserves to be looked at. It may be that he or she is willing to invest in your idea as an expression of support. Presumably, you will have established that this support is there during your initial assessment of the various aspects of the business.

From both your points of view, it may make sense as a means of avoiding borrowing elsewhere which you may be ill able to afford.

parents, relatives or friends

Money provided from any of these sources must be accompanied with the assurance that you will be left to run the business in the way you see fit. Anyone who invests in your business must be convinced that it is a realistic proposition; otherwise, they would not invest. You should make it clear to them that they are not buying a say in the business.

It should also be made clear to them when they can expect to see their money returned. An agreement should be drawn up by a solicitor if the amount to be loaned is considerable, though you will probably each have to use a separate solicitor to do this.

loans

Some lenders use the PARTS formula to help them assess whether or not to grant a loan. Even those who may not use the formula *per se* will use its criteria:

■ What is the *Purpose* of the loan?
■ What is the *Amount* being asked for?
■ What will be the *Repayment* period?
■ What will be the *Terms* (the profit potential to the lender)?
■ What *Security* is there?

This last refers not only to your contribution and collateral, but to your character and management ability.

bank loans

Most banks offer special arrangements for new and small business, and specific details can be had on request.

There are several types of bank loan that have direct relevance to a start-up or new business. Though the precise details may differ, some examples are:

1. *Business Development Loan.* Short-, medium- or long-term (usually larger) loan for growing businesses. Usually repayable up to 20 years.
2. *Overdraft.* Always an option and should generally be used for short-term working capital. Theoretically, an overdraft is always repayable on demand.

3. *Personal loan.* Though not strictly a business loan, a great many small businesses do resort to this route to finance their idea, perhaps because other routes are closed to them.

4. *Loan Guarantee Scheme.* This is a government-backed loan scheme designed to offer financial help to those starting small businesses whose business plan shows their idea to be viable but who have no security or track record that could help them obtain a loan. The DTI guarantees 70 per cent of the outstanding amount due to the lender (rising to 85 per cent for businesses that have been trading for two years or more at the time of the application) over 2 to 10 years in return for a premium on the guaranteed portion of the loan. The limit on loans is presently £250,000 for an existing business. For a new business the limit is £100,000. For this purpose a 'new' business is defined as being in existence for two years or less. An existing business is defined as being in existence for two years or more.

League tables showing the extent to which each lender is supporting the LGS should be available from the DTI, and these will provide useful guidelines to small businesses in planning which lenders to approach. Lenders currently in the scheme include the Allied Irish Bank, the Bank of Ireland, the Bank of Scotland, Barclays Bank, Clydesdale Bank, First Trust Bank, HSBC Bank, 3i Group plc, Lloyds TSB, the London Enterprise Agency, National Westminster Bank, Northern Bank, Northern Venture Managers Ltd, the Royal Bank of Scotland, the Ulster Bank, the Yorkshire Bank and Yorkshire Enterprise Ltd. You can obtain more information from DTI regional offices or your local Business Link. You may also write to the DTI Loan Guarantee Section, Level 2, St Mary's House, c/o Moorfoot, Sheffield S1 4PQ or ring the Section on 0114 259 730819; fax 0114 259 7316, e-mail sflgs@sbs.gsi.gov.uk.

the bank in perspective

As with all businesses, banks are first and foremost there to make a profit. They wish to do this at minimal risk. A bank can sell you insurance policies, pensions and investment schemes but, in the final analysis, it primarily sells money to make money. It is a money shop.

The bank manager is a money shop manager and, while he or she deserves respect, must be seen in that light. You are a customer, there to buy the money he or she is selling, and to compare that bank's terms with the terms of other money shops. He or she will be judging not just your proposition, but you. You should judge not just the bank manager's proposition, but him or her. Is the manager the kind of person you will feel comfortable dealing with?

Not only will you need to show that you have given considerable care to the structure or your business plan, and be able to put up a fair proportion of the capital required yourself, but you may be asked to provide security against any monies that you are allowed to borrow. This security will take the form of an asset, usually your home. Should it prove necessary, the bank will sell your home (if this is the security) and deduct what is owed to them.

Therefore, at no point should you feel that the bank manager is doing you a favour by granting you a loan or an overdraft, if he or she chooses to. The manager has made a considered business judgement and believes that you are a safe enough prospect to make a profit from.

You in return should judge the bank manager and the deal he or she is offering you. Bear in mind the following points:

- ■ Does the manager have the authority to grant the loan you are requesting?
- ■ There is no point in dealing with a sub-branch if it means they cannot make this decision themselves. Go to the main local branch instead.

- Make sure that the manager or adviser is genuinely involved in what you are saying, maybe even making suggestions that hadn't occurred to you.
- Believe that the bank would like to help you, and accept that they will want to clarify a few things first.
- Be friendly and professional, without compromising yourself.
- Be well prepared, ready to talk and confident. Be able to take some initiative yourself.
- The interview ritual, properly conducted, will be a dignified mutual transaction under defined circumstances.
- Despite having inside knowledge of business, the bank manager has probably never actually gone out there and set up a business – and probably never will.
- Send your business plan into the bank manager a few days before your appointment so that he or she can digest it in advance.
- If you want to go that extra mile – and you should – do a second set of financial forecasts with (say) 25 per cent *less* sales turnover. If you are lucky enough to have a computer spreadsheet, then this will prove a simple enough exercise. Otherwise it will be more time-consuming. It will be worth doing because, first, you will foresee what would happen if you failed to meet your targets, and second, your lender will be impressed by your thoroughness.

finance companies

Finance companies are secondary lenders. This means that they borrow the money which they in turn lend to you. Once they have covered their own borrowing costs and then added in their profit element, they will usually prove one of the more expensive options.

building societies

Building societies are not keen to lend for business. That said, and referring again to the fact that many new and small businesses do turn to the personal loan as a means of financing their enterprise, as long as you can qualify for a personal loan from this source, what you do with it afterwards is, effectively, your business.

venture capital

Venture capital is capital raised through the sale of equity in your business. One in 20 who present their business plans to a venture capitalist will be accepted as a suitable investment. You need to be aware that you will not just be accepting a loan, if it is granted; the investor will expect to be actively involved in your company and its progress.

You will need to take advice on whether or not your business is the kind that a venture capitalist would be interested in. The first stage would be to see your local Business Link. For details of the nearest Business Link, phone the signpost line on 0845 600 9006, or access their Web site at www.businesslink.org.

A Directory of Sources of Venture Capital under £250,000 is available from The Stationery Office (TSO – formerly HMSO prior to privatisation in 1996) bookshops and accredited agents, which should be listed in the *Yellow Pages* under 'Booksellers'. Otherwise, contact HMSO Publications Centre, for distance orders only. The address is PO Box 276, London SW8 5DT, or log on at www.hmso.gov.uk.

The British Venture Capital Association, Essex House, 12–13 Essex Street, London WC2R 3AA (tel: 020 7240 3846; Web site www.bvca.co.uk) provides information about members to those seeking venture capital funding. You can obtain the *BVCA Directory of Members* and a useful *Guide to Venture Capital* on request and at no cost to you.

The Business Expansion Scheme, which promoted individual investment in small or growing businesses, ended in December 1993 but the Confederation of British Industry (CBI) and other groups lobbying on behalf of small companies pushed for an improved version of the outgoing scheme, tentatively named The Smaller Companies Investment Scheme. As a result of this lobbying, many of the ideas put forward were absorbed by the government into what is now the Enterprise Investment Scheme, which replaced BES from January 1994. More information is available on www.eisa.org.org.uk.

Accountants, stockbrokers and solicitors may also have contacts with wealthy individuals in the community who are looking for suitable businesses in which to invest.

government and European Union schemes and grants

We have already touched upon the government's Loan Guarantee Scheme (see p 65).

It is often possible to obtain current information on sources of grants and loans from chartered accountants. This area is well worth researching as it is greatly underused. There are also several relevant directories that could be inspected at your nearest business library. See 'Directories' on p. 151.

This is a complex area and takes time to research, but your local Business Link is there to help and advise.

the Prince's Youth Business Trust

If you are about to set up in business and are unemployed and aged between 18 and 30 years inclusive, The Prince's Youth Business Trust will be able to offer you advice, and may be able to offer financial assistance. This financial assistance could be:

■ 'soft' loans of up to £5,000 (average £2,000);
■ a grant of up to £1,500 per person, or £3,000 if there are two or more people involved in the business;
■ grants of up to £250 per business which can be used for market research.

You can also access:

■ a volunteer business mentor;
■ self-help kits and free advice;
■ exhibitions.

No qualifications are needed, and the Trust welcomes applications from young offenders, members of minority groups and young people with disabilities. You will only need to show that you have the ability and determination to succeed in the business you have chosen.

The Prince's Youth Business Trust is at 18 Park Square East, London NW1 4LH (tel: 020 7543 1234; textphone: 020 7543 1374). To find your nearest Prince's Trust office, go to the main Web site on www.princes-trust.org.uk, then click on 'go regional'.

credit unions

Credit unions, for unfathomable reasons, are not usually mentioned as sources of finance. Perhaps this is because, as the movement itself puts it, they are the country's 'best-kept secret'.

A credit union is a 'not-for-profit' financial cooperative which must be legally registered under the Credit Unions Act 1979 and is regulated by the Financial Services Authority (FSA). Credit union members can borrow at 12.68 per cent APR (annual percentage rate or 'true' rate, as opposed to the 'flat' rate, which can be misleading). You pay a small fee to join – usually £1 – and there are no hidden charges. The 12.68 per cent APR is the maximum rate a credit union is allowed to charge; larger credit unions can offer even lower rates.

The credit union movement started in 1849 in Germany, and since then has spread to more than 80 countries world-wide, with in excess of 100 million members. There are now over 700 credit unions in Great Britain alone (ie not including Northern Ireland's flourishing credit unions) with a member-ship of between 250,000 and 350,000 depending on which source you consult.

Though the majority of credit unions tend to be community based, there are also work-based and associational credit unions. Of the community-based credit unions – most of which are still run almost entirely by volunteers – Leeds City Credit Union is one of the largest, while of the work-based credit unions Glasgow Council Credit Union is notable. The police have their own credit union, as do London taxi drivers and companies such as British Airways. A good example of an associational credit union is that run for the members of the Federation of Small Businesses.

Though larger credit unions in Britain are now equal in size to the smaller building societies, there is still immense potential for growth. In the nearby Republic of Ireland, for example, there is a credit union on every main street, and between a third and a half of the population there are credit union mem-bers. Dublin County alone boasts more than 120 credit unions, most actually competing on lending and dividend rates.

Since joining the regulatory regime of the Financial Services Authority (FSA) in July 2002, British credit unions now bene-fit from the Financial Services Compensation Scheme. This means that members have the same level of consumer protec-tion as depositors with banks and building societies.

If there is a credit union in your area, you will be required to save with it as a member for three months before you are allowed to apply for a loan. This is to ensure that you are not borrowing beyond your means and that you have the discipline to pay regular amounts of money into your account. Depending on which credit union you are with, you may be paid a dividend of between 1.5 and 8 per cent on your savings.

The ethos of a credit union is to help ensure that its members learn thrift and good money management, and, where credit is supplied, that this should be 'credit with dignity'.

To find out whether there is a credit union in your area, or for more information generally, contact the Association of British Credit Unions Ltd on 0161 832 3694, Web site www.abcul.org, or check your local directories.

setting up: the business structure

We now need to consider the various ways in which a new business may be established. Your choice will be influenced by the nature of your business and to a lesser extent by your own nature. The main possibilities are sole trader, partnership or limited company.

sole trader

If you intend to set up alone, and it is not likely that your house or any other personal possessions will be put at risk, you will probably become a sole trader.

The sole trader is the simplest form of business start-up, and will be the best course to take if your business is to be a straightforward affair such as a self-employed tradesman or market trader.

You regard income from the business as your personal income, and pay personal rate income tax on it, after business expenses have been offset. You need to keep good business records to justify such expenses in case these are queried by the Inland Revenue. You must inform your tax office that you are starting up in business. You can do this by calling 08459 154515. Sole traders pay Class 2 and Class 4 National Insurance contributions. Class 2 is a flat rate, adjusted annually; Class 4 is a percentage of profits.

The Inland Revenue (IR) are far more user-friendly than you might think, and are a good source of practical help not just for new businesses but for those who are still thinking about starting up or becoming self-employed.

If you phone the number above, you can ask for a free copy of the IR's video *Starting Up in Business*. You can also ask to be sent the *Starting Up in Business Guide*, which covers things like how to get off to a good start, the basics of income tax, National Insurance, VAT, tax credits and allowances, and how to get further help. If you're already up and running, you can ask for an adviser from one of the IR's Business Support Teams to call and give you advice on record-keeping, filling in and filing tax returns, what to do when you take someone on, and so on.

The Business Support Teams even run local workshops specifically for people starting self-employment and – best of all – it's all free of charge.

Find out from your local council if any licence is required for the business you plan to start. Local rules can vary, so it is not possible to give details here.

The main disadvantage with setting up as a sole trader is that your liability will not be limited. This should not be a problem if you do not anticipate a high element of risk that would leave you exposed financially.

The term 'sole trader' is derived from the fact that you, under that business structure, would be solely responsible for the running of the business, for taking its profits and for suffering its losses, if applicable.

Despite its name, sole trading does allow you to have employees. They will be under your management and you will still have sole responsibility for the operation of the firm. The employment costs can be set against your income as a business expense.

You can start in business as a sole trader, and later take on partners or become a limited company.

partnership

Like a sole trader, a business partnership of two or more people can be set up quite straightforwardly, with minimal legal complications. Once you have told the tax office of your intention, and checked with the local council as already advised, you may begin trading on the date chosen. Partners pay personal income tax, like a sole trader, as well as Class 2 and Class 4 National Insurance contributions.

The Companies Act 1985 allows partnerships between solicitors, stockbrokers and accountants to number more than 20, but otherwise a partnership will consist of between 2 and 20 people. A partnership exists in the eyes of the law when two or more people carry on business in common with a view to making a profit.

As with a sole trader, any letterheads must carry the names of the partners involved in the business, and an address at which documents could be served if necessary. This also applies to orders, invoices, receipts and demands.

Ask yourself first of all, is it really necessary to have a partner or partners? Can you start up the business without them?

A partnership should be very carefully considered before being entered into. You need to trust everyone you are taking on as a partner because any one partner in a firm may make a contract that is legally binding on the remaining partners, and this trust is open to abuse. Partners are individually responsible for all the liabilities of the partnership, even if they were incurred without their knowledge, so a great element of mutual trust is involved.

The best form of partnership can be that of husband and wife, perhaps because they are already accustomed to sharing pressures. You would need to be certain that the extra time together under a business regime would not put strain on the marriage, however.

If your partner or partners are friends with whom you get on well, this friendship will not automatically carry over into the more serious arena of business. Even a partnership formed purely for professional reasons, where someone with sales ability, for example, enters into partnership with another who is a manufacturer, may be best avoided. Though relevant issues can be covered in the partnership deed, the very fact that this deed is required is itself indicative of the extra strains partnerships can bring.

The partnership deed should be drafted by or with the help of a solicitor and should set down the following matters in legally binding terms:

1. The start date of the partnership, the nature and place of its business, and whether or not other business beyond the main business can be carried on.
2. The length of holidays due and what other time, if any, will be allowed off, and what will be the consequences should any partner be absent for a period that exceeds the time off agreed.
3. More generally, under what circumstances should it be possible to expel a partner from the partnership or allow a new partner to join.
4. Will all partners have equal voting rights?
5. It will be necessary to define what is meant by 'voting decisions' and 'policy'.
6. Duties will need to be clearly defined and allocated between the partners.
7. It might be advisable to make it a term of the partnership deed that cheques and contracts over a certain amount be brought to the attention of all partners before they can be authorised.
8. How profits and losses are to be shared will need to be defined.
9. A limit will need to be set on each partner's weekly, monthly or yearly drawings.

10. A decision as to how long the partnership will last will need to be taken, perhaps with a notice period included for anyone who wishes to leave.
11. It should be noted that in the case of a partner leaving, all customers and suppliers of the partnership should be notified in writing of this fact. Failure to do this would mean that not only would that leaving partner remain responsible for the partnership debts, but the partnership would be responsible for any debts that the leaving partner subsequently built up.
12. How to allot a share of capital to a departing partner.
13. Partners will need to decide how books are to be kept and by what outside firm, if not the partnership itself.

Partnership deeds will cost time and money to prepare, but should be given the closest consideration by all parties concerned. This document will act as the rule book should issues ever become blurred in the future. All eventualities should be anticipated as thoroughly as possible.

The partnership deed, if put in place, overrides the Partnership Act 1890, which would otherwise be enforceable at law. The above points should be included where relevant along with others pertinent to your precise situation. The list I have provided is intended to act as a guide and a spur rather than as a definitive statement of what should be included.

sleeping, general and limited partnerships

A partnership might work best if there are two people involved, one of whom is a sleeping partner. This would mean that the latter partner's part in the business would be as an investor only, thus causing minimum interference.

It is interesting that although the partnership in the context of the company will not have limited liability, the sleeping partner(s) may if they so choose have 'limited partnerships': their capital is at risk but nothing else that they own.

In any situation where a business chooses the partnership structure, however, at least one of the partners involved must be a 'general partner' with unlimited liability.

partnership and self-assessment

Each partner will now pay tax on their share of the profits. Thus, the partnership's returns must show how the profit (or loss) is split between each partner. One welcome change is that partners will no longer have to pay tax on a defaulting partner's share. See page 82 for sources of information.

the limited company

A limited company is recognised in law as a separate entity from the individuals who own it and separate from the individuals who make its decisions – the shareholders and directors respectively. The company is perceived as running its own business.

Therefore, as an entity that is separate from the individuals involved, it is responsible for its own debts, and liability for them is limited to the company itself. To anyone running or owning a limited liability company, this means that only the value of their shares will be lost should the company fail, and not their home or other assets unless they have given personal guarantees.

Shareholders appoint directors, and can appoint themselves as directors, and the rights and responsibilities of both shareholders and directors will be clearly set out in the articles of association, which is the limited company's version of the partnership deed. As with the partnership deed, you would do well to bring in the expertise of a solicitor to help with the articles of association.

The limited company will also need to be registered with the Registrar of Companies, a process with which the same solicitor could help. Alternatively, you could contact a firm that specialises in company registration, and compare respective charges before deciding who to use. The *Yellow Pages* will prove useful to you in this instance.

Your company will be registered at Companies House, as will your registered office address and (once you are up and running) your annual accounts. Your part in this process should be confined to signing forms when advised, unless you choose to prepare and submit the necessary documentation yourself, which you are of course allowed to do in law.

The documentation submitted to Companies House will include:

- memorandum of association;
- articles of association;
- statement of capital on formation;
- statement of first directors and secretary and address of the registered office;
- declaration of compliance with the law with reference to the Companies Acts.

Once all is in order, you will be sent your certificate of incorporation. The limited company now exists and you can begin trading.

You will need to decide with your accountant what date the incorporated company will use as its year-end for accounts purposes, and Companies House will need to be informed of this.

Unlike a sole trader or a partnership, a limited liability company will have details of its address, shares, shareholders and directors, as well as its audited annual accounts on record and for public scrutiny at Companies House.

Company accounts must be audited by an independent, qualified auditor. Not all company accounts have to be audited as some may qualify for exemption, if this is applied for. These could include dormant companies and some 'small' companies. Because these things are always subject to change, you'd best check with Companies House by either going to their Web site on www.companies-house.gov.uk or phoning them on 0870 3333636.

However, as a guide, the situation at time of writing was that to obtain the right to be exempt from audit, a small company must:

■ qualify as 'small' according to criteria that include the number of employees;
■ have a turnover of not more than £1 million;
■ have a balance sheet of not more than £1.4 million.

Charitable companies are governed by a separate set of rules, so you'll need to check what these are if you classify your company under this heading.

Directors of limited companies are now classed as PAYE employees and are not able to benefit from being assessed as self-employed for tax purposes.

The company must have at least one shareholder who acts as director.

Company stationery must include company name, address and the registration number. Although the company can still be 'trading as' under a name different from its registered name, the company stationery must indicate that it is 'limited'.

Setting-up costs are incurred by limited companies. As mentioned above, annual accounts must be audited by an independent, qualified accountant or auditor, and a set of specified documents submitted annually to Companies House. Companies pay corporation tax on profits.

cooperatives

There are a number of different kinds of cooperative including, for example, equity participation, worker and community cooperatives, but these are comparatively rare forms of business start-up.

Information can be obtained from the Industrial Common Ownership Movement (ICOM), Holyoake House, Hanover Street, Manchester M60 0AS (tel: 0161 246 2959). Their Web sit can be accessed by linking from www.co-op.co.uk or through their financial arm, which is Industrial Common Ownership Finance, www.icof.co.uk.

value added tax

All businesses must register for VAT once their annual turnover exceeds the sum announced annually in the Budget. They must charge VAT to customers and pass the tax on to Customs and Excise. Their own VAT payments can be reclaimed if they are registered.

It should be noted that the phrase 'annual turnover' as used in this context does not refer to either the accounting year or the calendar year. 'Annual turnover', in this instance, means 12 months backwards from the present; that is, it is what is termed a 'rolling year'.

Zero-rated goods (which include food, books and newspapers, drugs and medicines) have a nil rate of VAT imposed on sales to customers, even though the manufacturers will be charged VAT on raw materials used to produce them. There are also 11 categories of VAT-exempt goods and services.

Retailers or anyone who handles a large number of cash transactions rather than issuing invoices with VAT added have the choice of various VAT-reporting schemes, and will use the most suitable for their particular business.

Full details are available from your local Customs and Excise Office, which will issue you with explanatory leaflets. Registered businesses and individuals are kept informed of changes by means of a regular newsletter.

record-keeping

It will be obvious from the above that in order to comply with the VAT regulations and Inland Revenue requirements, meticulous business records must be kept, either by yourself or by a bookkeeper/accountant. The penalties for non-compliance can be severe and/or expensive.

You will need to keep the following records as a minimum:

1. *Cash book*
   (a) Record cash sales and payments made from cash transactions
   (b) Record payments in and out of the bank
   (c) Show VAT on payments as applicable
2. *VAT records* (if applicable)
   (a) Show how VAT return figures have been calculated
   (b) In addition, non-retailers must maintain a list of sales invoices issued
3. *Petty cash book* (where applicable)
   Small cash expenses should be kept on an imprest basis and should show VAT where applicable
4. *Wages book, wage slips*
   Summary information to meet the needs of the employee and the Inland Revenue
5. *Order and delivery books*
   Purchases and sales, orders and deliveries
6. *Overdue accounts book*
   Debtors and age analysis of debts for all credit sales.

Professional advice from your accountant should establish the most appropriate records for the business. If you follow the accountant's advice, it will also tend to reduce his or her fees.

useful sources of information

1. Start with the Web site www.businesslink.org.
2. The official Web site of the Treasury is www. hm-treasury.gov.uk. It provides up-to-the-minute pages of budget news, new initiatives and guidance for SMEs.
3. The Inland Revenue Web site can be found at www.inlandrevenue.gov.uk. It provides help on how

to fill in self-assessment returns as well as the latest budget news.
4. The Customs and Exercise 'National Advice Service' can be contacted on 0845 010 9000, or access the Web site on www.hmce.gov.uk.

premises

Working from home

We have already looked at working from home in Chapter 1. Many start-up businesses, by their nature or size, cannot take this as an option. This chapter will consider the other possibilities.

Probably the first point to make is that any other option you choose is likely to cost more than working from home. Not only will there be the cost of travel to work, but also buying or leasing property will cost money. There will also be such expenses as insurance, rates, repairs and perhaps furniture.

For obvious reasons, the home is very often first choice of premises for the self-employed. Increasingly, employees too are given, or are asking for, the option of doing their duties from home. Where this is the case, the employee is often sub-contracted as a separate business. This strategy can increase productivity by up to 100 per cent.

Advances in telecommunications have meant that it is just as easy to work from a computer terminal at home as it is to work from a city centre office. For further information, contact the Telework, Telecottage and Telecentre Association (TCA) on 0800 616008 or access their Web site, wwwtelework.org.uk.

Telecottages are countryside nerve centres fully equipped with modern computer and communication technology and funded by various sources among which are local councils, the European Social Fund and Rural Development Funds.

In June 2002 the BBC reported that more than 2 million people in the United Kingdom work from home for at least part of the time. This was an increase of more than two-thirds on comparable figures from 1997. About 43 per cent of these workers were self-employed.

location

Before deciding on the premises, you will need to choose the location, taking into account the needs of your business.

It is usual for new businesses to start up in the area in which the founder lives. There is even a school of thought that says that it is ill-advised to start a new business and move to an unknown area at the same time.

However, each case has its own constraints, which will influence where the business is best located. You may only need storage space, which means that you need only rent a lock-up garage.

If you are in a partnership, it may be possible to use your partner's home. You could also look at sharing an office, factory or industrial unit with another business. You will need to be sure the lease allows this, though.

Check with your local Business Link whether there are designated areas locally that receive financial aid or grants. Such aid will be from the European Union, central government (the Department of Trade and Industry) or local authorities, and geographical location will often have a bearing.

There are perhaps 50 or so enterprise zones in the UK, and these are exempt from rates and almost free from planning controls. One hundred per cent capital allowances are available on the construction or extension of property within the zones. Check with your local authority to see if there are enterprise zones in your area.

There are also assisted areas run by English Partnerships, often offering simple tenancy agreements and industrial and commercial property on flexible terms. English Partnerships can be contacted on www.englishpartnerships.com.

an answering service or a business centre?

An answering service will take incoming messages on your behalf, and give a response which you will have agreed. You could choose to have a pager so that wherever you are, you could be informed of calls as they come in so that you can respond quickly.

Alternatively, the answering service could tell the caller that you are expected to make contact at noon, and could they take the caller's number so that you can phone them then. Obviously, you could use a mobile phone but this would not usually be your main contact number.

Business centres are a natural progression from this, offering a complete office facility. For a very reasonable fee, a business centre can act as your business address for mailing and your answering service. You might choose to pay for only those two services, or you might opt to use its secretarial service, which would include all modern equipment such as word processors, faxes, telexes, photocopiers, e-mail and Internet facilities.

A business centre will also be able to rent you an office on a full-time, part-time or even hourly basis. It can also allow you to hire a boardroom for presentations, and even have the coffee and refreshments brought in.

As you pay for only what you choose to use, you can put across an impressive image at minimal cost. You will find such services advertised in your local paper, the *Thomson Directory* and the *Yellow Pages* under 'Business Centres'. You can also find 'virtual offices' on the Net if you just type (say) 'answering service, UK' into a search engine.

retail premises

In retailing, success is said to depend on three factors: location, location and location. Even being at the wrong end of the main street can mean tipping the scales against yourself in such an instance.

If you are considering selling anything from a shop, the only way to fully establish whether or not the premises you have in mind are suitable is to conduct extensive on-site research. This should include parking nearby at differing times of day on different days of the week, and simply counting the human traffic that actually steps across the threshold. Furthermore, you should observe carefully how many of these people leave the premises with a purchase.

Of course, passing trade will be a key factor in any retail operation, so you will need to make yourself aware of just how heavy or light the pedestrian traffic is:

■ Are there more pedestrians on the other side of the street, or is 'your' side busier?

■ Are the retail premises you are considering positioned so as to catch their eye, entice them to pause and then enter?

■ If there are no pedestrians, but a good flow of vehicular traffic, is it easy for a driver both to notice the premises in good time, and pull over and park without difficulty?

■ Are enough of them doing this?

■ Can you discover any reason why the flow of trade should be disrupted in the future? For example, are there plans to build a bypass nearby? Are the premises licensed to trade as they are doing? Is there any reason to suspect that there will be increased competition soon? Is the street to be changed to one-way traffic or have a yellow line put down it?

■ Are there any bus queues, train or bus stations, supermarkets, YMCAs, theatres, cinemas, football grounds or car parks nearby that might affect trade at certain times of the day, or on certain days of the week?

■ Will any of the above be closing or expanding in the foreseeable future?

■ In the final analysis, do customers find the premises handy, and would they like you to offer an associated service or product that would mean them spending more? Ask them.

While we are on the subject of retailing, if it is to be a mobile shop you will need to consult your local authority to see if a licence is required. This will also be the case with a market stall. A delivery van from which food was sold would come under the regulations applying to market stalls.

You will certainly need a permit to operate in the street, and you cannot simply drive and park where you choose, ideal as this would be. The police would also need to be consulted, preferably before you have bought a vehicle, as the restrictions on where you could park and trade may strongly affect your decision.

Even if your customers will only need to visit your premises occasionally, location will have an effect in a number of ways:

■ It may be important that the address on your stationery is in a credible location. You must have an address appropriate to what you are selling. If you are to deal in quality cars, even if they are not new, customers will not lend you much credibility if you are based in a shabbier part of town.

■ If the rates are particularly high, it will mean your having to add these in to your costings, and this may make your unit or hourly cost uncompetitive.

■ If there are too many 'For Sale' signs about, you would do well to wonder why. Is there a high crime rate in the area? Is it difficult to trade for any other reason? Ask surrounding businesses.

Depending on whether you will be leasing or buying premises, other considerations will be:

■ The time it will take you to travel to work and back.

■ The cost of this travel.

■ The availability or otherwise of suitable parking space.

■ Proximity to the station.

■ If you will be employing staff now or in the future, is the area well served by public transport?

■ If you will be stocking heavy goods or installing machinery, is the floor strong enough?

■ Will there be enough space on the premises for the amount of stock you will be carrying and for fork-lift trucks at full working height if these are to be used?

■ Is the building in a good state of repair with all services such as power, water and phone points laid on?

■ What kind of insurance will the premises need and who will be responsible for paying this?

■ What security is there? Does this security restrict your business in any way?

■ Will you need a surveyor to check there is no subsidence?

■ If you are to be an accountant, a designer, a copywriter or to offer a service that requires long periods of concentration, you will need low noise levels. See the premises during the working week so that noise from nearby factories, traffic, aircraft, schools and other businesses can be checked.

■ Will the premises need much spending on them to make them habitable and who will be responsible for this?

■ You will be either renting or buying a property from which to work, and all will involve an outlay. If this figure is different from the one you used in your business plan, you will need to adjust that and assess the knock-on effect. Can you still afford it, or should you lower your sights?

leasing premises

Most new small businesses will lease premises rather than buy them. As it is less expensive, it will help your cash flow.

Once you have determined the location and size of the premises you require, it should not take long to narrow down your choice and obtain a copy of the relevant lease. Before signing this, take it to a business adviser at your local Business Link and obtain a list of points to query, which you can then take to a solicitor. Some of the principal points you may need to clarify are:

■ When is the first rent review due? This could create an increase in outgoings that you will need to foresee.
■ Are there any options to terminate the lease on either side?
■ Is the person who is offering the lease authorised to do so?
■ Will you in turn be authorised to sell the lease on should you choose to?
■ Do the terms of the lease allow you to sublet any part of the premises?
■ If the lease is near its end, will you be allowed to renew it? And on what terms?
■ Is there an option to purchase the premises written into the terms of the lease?
■ If there are extensive repairs to be done to the property, and the lease holds you responsible, can you obtain a reduction in the financial commitment to reflect this?
■ If the lease is a new lease, you will need to ensure that you are released from all obligations when you sell the lease on, otherwise any subsequent tenant's backlog of rent could end up being your responsibility.

Many of the checks listed under 'Buying premises' (below) apply here too, and the intricacy of the lease document will need to be examined by a solicitor. The points made here are guidelines only and not necessarily comprehensive.

With a lease you may be expected to pay a lump sum down as well as the regular payments agreed.

The Landlord and Tenant Act 1954, Part II, lays down the rights and obligations of business landlords towards their tenants, and vice versa. Certain procedures must be followed prior to a tenant being given notice to vacate the premises, and the main thrust of the Act is to provide security of tenure to the tenant, given that he or she complies with its terms.

buying premises

Buying premises is not the usual route for a small business start-up, but should be looked at in case you are in a position to consider this.

Five points you will need to keep in mind:

- If the premises are a new building or must undergo a 'change of use', you will need to consult your local authority planning department.

- Any factory, office or shop with more than 20 employees, or more than 10 not at ground level, needs a fire certificate from the fire department. If you do not fall into this category, but store highly flammable materials or explosives, you should also consult your local fire department as you may need a fire certificate.

- The same applies to a hotel or boarding house with sleeping accommodation for more than six people or any guests or staff sleeping above first floor or below ground level.

- If the premises will need any structural alterations, you must consult the planning department of the local authority, the building regulations department, the fire brigade, the water board and the sewerage undertakers.

■ You are best advised to employ a solicitor to effect the purchase, and have the property surveyed by a surveyor.

It may be possible, if you have insufficient capital or believe it is better not to over-commit yourself, to arrange a commercial mortgage with a bank or building society. If you choose to enter into this kind of arrangement, you should feel easy in your own mind that the repayments will not tie up too much of your cash flow. Keep in mind that you will need working capital to allow for anticipated troughs and for the unforeseen.

Refer to your business plan again, and ensure that you do not over-commit yourself in this area. At this early stage, outgoings will be heavy enough without succumbing to the temptation of premises that are unnecessarily lavish for this stage of your business. As a realistic precaution, reforecast the effect of sales turnover being 25 per cent less than expected. Could you, in such circumstances, afford the rent or commercial mortgage you are proposing to pay? Your first consideration should be to secure adequate premises with a minimal cost.

Possible advantages of buying premises are:

■ Once equity has built up, premises may be used as collateral to obtain a loan for expansion in the future.
■ Owning the premises from which you trade can mean that you are perceived as being solid and permanent.
■ Ownership improves the value of your company.
■ If you own the premises outright or pay a fixed-rate mortgage, you will suffer no unpredictable increases in rent.
■ It is likely to be easier to sell the property if and when you need to, as opposed to selling a lease.
■ The fact that you are committing yourself to purchasing the premises means that you really are totally committed to your business.

local authorities, councils and development organisations

As with finance, grants, and business advice generally, your local authority will often be a good starting point for advice on finding property. A specialised property matching service will sometimes be provided by the estates department of the council. This will consist of a database that is updated on a regular basis, thus providing you with instant and comprehensive information. This database is likely to cover industrial and commercial sites as well as office premises both for sale and lease.

Great Britain is now well served by a good number of regional development agencies (RDAs) across England, Wales and Scotland. These will often have a network of sub-offices or regional divisions. You will need to check where your nearest contact point is, but here is a helpful list to be going on with:

- One NorthEast (tel: 0191 261 2000);
- North West Development Agency (tel: 01925 400 100);
- Yorkshire Forward (tel: 0113 243 9222);
- Advantage West Midlands (tel: 0121 380 3500);
- East Midlands Development Agency (tel: 0115 988 8300);
- East of England Development Agency (tel: 01223 713 900);
- South West of England Regional Development Agency (tel: 01392 214 747);
- SEEDA (based in Guildford; tel: 01483 484 226);
- London Development Agency (tel: 0207 954 4646);
- Welsh Development Agency (tel: 0845 777 5577);
- Scottish Enterprise Network (helpline 0845 607 8787).

RDAs were set up in April 1999 as 'powerhouses' for regeneration in the regions, and you may find that your RDA is helpful in signposting you towards 'easy-in, easy-out' business premises for start-ups. Variously known as 'managed workspaces', 'enterprise centres' or 'small business centres', these are often available on monthly terms, at competitive rates and (sometimes) with centralised administrative facilities offering maximum convenience with minimum fuss or commitment.

Whereas when one is working from home, there is the risk of a feeling of isolation, this risk is lessened when your business is among others in similar circumstances. The nearness and sense of a shared mission will provide a welcome stimulus.

As well as the advantage of having access to preferential lease arrangements, having your own business in a local authority block means you will often also have the following:

■ a shared receptionist and secretary, which gives a much more professional front to your company, and enables you to have your messages taken even when you're not there;

■ a shared photocopier;

■ an answerphone facility for calls made outside office hours;

■ the possibility of doing business with other proprietors like yourself;

■ the likelihood of there being minimal costs and outlay for the arrangement.

As part of an overall strategy to cut red tape, local authorities have been asked to cut planning delays and to lessen the need for planning applications.

useful reference points to help with your search

Probably the most obvious place to find premises for rent or sale is the local newspaper. Local libraries will usually have the latest copy of this and will also be able to advise you of any reference books or directories that would help you in your search.

Precise details of your requirements should be given to any agency you choose to make use of. Arranging office furniture, removals and any of the details involved would be best undertaken by yourself to avoid a premium on the cost.

marketing, selling and promotion

The bridge between your business and your potential customer is the selling function. This is an area in which many start-ups feel weak.

Since it is a first priority for any new business to generate and then to capitalise upon leads, that responsibility must be accepted and the task approached constructively and firmly.

You will need to consider how to market your company and how to sell its 'product'. Again, the term is used to mean product or service.

If you have the kind of product that can be sold by others on a commission basis, or if you have included a sales representative's wages in your costings, perhaps you can delegate the selling task. Or it may be that your product is the kind that can be sold by 'party plan', where a network of contacts arrange informal parties for their friends at which you have the opportunity to allow the interested group to inspect your product with a view to purchasing.

More often, however, the task will be wholly and entirely your own responsibility. This marketing and selling will be a continuous need, not just a temporary requirement. Even when up and running, you can expect to spend not less than 40 per cent of your time looking for new business.

Marketing and selling are two separate disciplines that have a shared objective: to attract the commitment of the buyer. Marketing, however, should begin prior to the 'product' being launched – which is why we studied it in part in Chapter 2.

It is the process whereby:

■ a market is identified;
■ its size anticipated;
■ its needs satisfied at a profit to the supplier.

Selling, on the other hand, is defined by the Institute of Sales and Marketing Management as 'the skill of making buying easy'. It is a separate function from marketing.

Since your 'product' has been invested with your skill and pride, it can be difficult to accept that the value of your contribution may not be readily recognised. In order to give it every chance of being recognised, you first need to ensure that sufficient potential customers are made aware of its existence. There are a number of means by which you can achieve this end, and we will look at some of them individually here. You must decide which is best for your particular case.

prior to start date

Even before you begin trading, you should already have begun to promote the fact and to have built up interest and clients or advance orders.

You can give details in advance to friends, relations, and those with whom you have worked, asking them to spread the word when they can. Ask your last employer for business.

You could use posters, where permitted, announcing your opening date and any activity relating to it.

If you are the kind of business that would benefit from advertising in directories such as the *Yellow Pages* or *Thomson Directory*, you will need to check the deadlines for their next editions so as to reserve your space. If you have a business telephone line, you are entitled to a line entry without charge, though you may feel that a boxed advertisement is more appropriate to you.

If you intend to have a wine and cheese party on your start date, or if the mayor will be in attendance, you could compose a press release for the local newspaper(s). It will, however, need to be newsworthy, as they are not in the habit of giving free advertisements. You need to think of a news angle that would attract their attention.

Although many trade and professional associations treat their list of members as confidential, you may be a member or acquainted with a member who will be happy to provide you with a copy. You can then send out a circular or an invitation to those on the list.

advertising

Ways of advertising can range from a postcard in your local shop windows, to radio and television campaigns. Obviously, if you only wish to sell your product locally, there is no point in advertising nationally.

Even excluding such options, you will be left with a wide choice. Check which medium the competition uses. This will probably be right for you. The choices can include:

- hand-delivered leaflets or brochures;
- parish bulletin advertisements;
- sandwich boards;
- leaflets enclosed in your local paper;
- bus or taxi advertisements;
- trade magazine and directory entries;
- exhibitions;
- cinema screens;
- personal calling;
- the Internet;
- text messaging.

Whichever type you choose, check that it is working by constantly asking customers where they heard of you, and keeping a record. This is imperative at the beginning, when you may have placed an advertisement in more than one publication or medium. Careful scrutiny will show you where your money is best spent.

If you will be preparing the advertisement yourself, think of how you can best convey your message. How can you make the advertisement stand out from the rest?

It is important to keep in mind the Trade Descriptions Acts 1968 and 1972, which leave you open to criminal charges if you describe your product or service falsely or make claims about it that are untrue. However, if you give careful consideration to your product and how it differs from the competition, you will uncover its unique selling point, which should allow you to describe it in glowing terms without needing to veer from the facts.

If you can portray what you do with the use of a motif or a simple sketch, this might more easily catch the reader's eye than a blur of words. A plastering firm might use the motif of a trowel, accompanied by the company name and telephone number, or a childminder might use a line drawing of a couple of toddlers hand-in-hand.

It should not be difficult to find a graphic designer in your area, who may be new in business too, and eager to foster your custom at a competitive rate. This may be a better route to designing your advertisement and business stationery than doing it yourself, if design is not one of your strengths.

This would be very good value if you were able to carry the design or logo across to packaging and company wear such as overalls. You might be able to use it for vehicle signage, helping to give a very professional 'corporate image' and inspiring confidence in your company.

using local papers

If you have a leaflet inserted in your local paper, you can either provide the leaflets to be enclosed, having paid for them to be printed elsewhere, or allow the paper itself to print and distribute the leaflet. The latter method may actually prove cheaper.

Although this can be more expensive than a straightforward advertisement in the newspaper itself, it will give you an even better chance of getting read. This method is probably most suited to a launch or some other such special event in the life of a business.

More usually, businesses advertise within the paper itself, and here there are a number of decisions to be made. First, if you can, cultivate a relationship with a journalist serving on the newspaper, feeding him or her newsworthy items that will help to promote your business.

Local papers, by their very nature, are interested in what is going on within the community, and often have a business section and an 'about town' section to be filled with interesting news items. So if you are doing a sponsored bungee jump for charity, will be offering employment to people when you open, or are the only person in your area with your particular qualifications, send off a press release saying so.

Alternatively, phone and ask for the news desk, who will be pleased to take notes on the spot, or pass you on to someone who will. In certain circumstances, they will even send a photographer.

This kind of public relations should be a continuous part of your business strategy, particularly considering the amount of money it would cost you to pay for advertising space that would equal that taken up by an article.

If there is more than just one local paper in your area, the surest way to find out which will give you the best response is to advertise in both and monitor the results.

If you choose not to take this course, do not just plump for the one with the lowest advertising rates, without first considering which is best for you. One of the newspapers will contain the most advertisements, and this is a good indication of which paper brings in the best results. You will also know by the editorial content and style which newspaper is the leader and which is the 'also-ran'.

Once you have decided which to advertise in, you must decide what size of advertisement will give you the best return. As likely as not, this will be strongly affected by your advertising budget. But even within this, you may have room for choice. Again, if it is possible, the only way to be sure is to try a number of different-sized advertisements and monitor the effect on response. You will have to decide whether you wish to place your advertisement in the classified section of the newspaper, or in the main section, or 'run of page'. The last option will be more costly but could be perceived as separating you from the competition.

In either case, the top right-hand corner of a right-hand-side page is said to be most likely to catch the reader's attention.

Whatever you decide in terms of design, wording, size and placing, your advertisement will have a better chance of working well for you if you run it over a number of weeks. If it is clear to you that you will be needing the advertisement on a regular basis, ask for a discount before giving this commitment. The good news is that most newspapers have an in-house studio or design department that will design your advertisement, as part of the package, free of charge.

the importance of selling

Start-ups, and even existing businesses – particularly those run by technicians or craftspeople with a non-selling background – may expect buyers to come to them, given the undoubted quality of what is on offer. This bunker mentality allows us to think of ourselves as managers rather than salespeople, but ignores the underlying fact that without sales there is nothing to manage.

Selling, therefore, is the very crux of any commercial under-taking and, if performed professionally and actively, will have the most dynamic influence on the growth of your company.

Advertisements will help in varying degrees, depending on your product. But just as marketing begins before you even start up in business, selling begins before the enquiries start coming in. Being proactive means you don't sit back and wait.

Depending on the number of new prospects to be contact-ed and the business you are in, you may choose between cold-calling (calling in person on strangers), a mailshot or a telephone-sales approach. A combination of the last two is especially effective.

the mailshot

There are agencies that will be happy to undertake the entire mailshot procedure from its inception through to the telesales follow-up. There are also freelance copywriters who could undertake the writing of the sales letter, or telesales companies that will be pleased to follow up the sales letter with a call. Perhaps you are starting up just such a service. However, not many businesses could afford to subcontract at this early stage, so it is worth examining the fundamentals involved in doing these things for yourself.

The objective of a mailshot is primarily to get the prospect to communicate with you. Your sales letter, therefore, must stress the benefits of your product to your prospect rather than simply extol its virtues. A device you can use to achieve this is the phrase 'which means that...'. To give an illustration, if you are a sign company that will be using colour-fast vinyl, a feature of your signs will be that *they will not fade*. To express this as a benefit for the prospective buyer, you need to use the phrase as indicated: 'The colour will not fade, which means that *there will be no maintenance costs*.'

When writing your sales letter, avoid beginning sentences with 'I', 'We' or 'Our', as these will make the construction sound self-centred. As a guideline, references to the prospect by use of the word 'you' should outnumber the self-centred words 'I', 'we' and 'our' by about two to one.

Break down your message into logically connected sections under sub-headings and use good quality stationery.

If you enclose a business reply card, opt for first-class post on it, as this will bring your reply in one day earlier, which could mean late this week rather than early next week.

To save using a code to monitor replies, have the prospect's details on the business reply card. This makes it straightforward to identify who is replying, and means the prospect does not have to fill in the details. Make it as easy as possible for him or her to respond. Selling, remember, is the skill of making buying easy.

You could choose to have a series of graded boxes to be ticked by the prospect to indicate the urgency of his or her requirement. This would enable you to order your response schedule correctly.

A typical business reply card might look like this:

                                                      Anyone
                                                      Any Firm
                                                    Anywhere

                                                  Please tick

I wish to place an order   ❏
I would like you to visit   ❏
I would like more information   ❏
Postage has been prepaid. Please post this card now.

Only send the sales letter (and business reply card if applicable) at this point, and use second-class stamps. It is normal to expect between 2 and 5 per cent response to a mailshot, so it is sensible to make a saving on postage here.

If you can afford company literature, do not send it indiscriminately. Await genuine enquiries, and qualify these. Keep trying to maximise income while minimising outgoings.

your mailshot list

Aside from the written content of your mailing, success will be markedly affected by the calibre of the list of sales prospects to be used. You can either compile the list yourself or purchase it from a list broker. As you will probably be hard pressed for time, you may consider it a good investment to purchase.

If you take that decision:

- Ask how often the list has been updated.
- Ask how many named contacts are included (ie not just company addresses).
- Consider how near to your base you will need the contact addresses to be – one estimate has it that 98 per cent of your business will be done within a 16-kilometre radius.

If you choose to build up your own list from classified directories at your library, you will need to confirm the managing director's name by telephone to the company concerned. Do not hesitate to clarify spellings as mistakes can cause offence, or at least indicate a lack of professionalism. This is because directories can be partly out of date even as they are published, because the necessary research began so long beforehand.

The extra cost incurred at this point is necessary as there is little virtue in having a list without contact names. The ability of direct mail to home in on an individual is a principal component of its strength. Also, this enables you to save postage by deleting those companies that are now defunct.

- Use window envelopes to avoid having to print the prospect's name twice – on the letter and on the envelope.

- ■ It is a good rule of thumb not to send out more mailings than you can follow up quickly by telephone.
- ■ 'Seed' each batch with a 'dummy' or two addressed to yourself so that you know when the mailshot has arrived.

A bite-sized personalised list of this sort will yield a higher response rate than the normal 2 to 5 per cent predicted by Post Office sources. Current wisdom has it that 30 per cent of your total response will be prompt while the remaining 70 per cent will trickle in.

Those who respond will expect an immediate reaction from you, and may not forgive delay, so if you cannot deal with each response as quickly as you would like, do write explaining that you have received their enquiry and will be contacting them soon. Do not leave them in the dark.

telephone selling

Once you have dealt with those who respond, you should use a prepared script to telephone those on your mailing list who did not respond. The telephone itself is a powerful selling tool, and the fact that you have already written to the managing director gives you a good introductory hinge.

Keep whatever information you have gathered on the company before you as you speak to help personalise the conversation, and ask a number of prepared questions about their company to develop their interest. Your objective, in this instance, might be to obtain a meeting to introduce your product. Offer a choice of two possible meeting dates, not less than one week ahead, to lessen the possibility of clashing with their schedule.

Monday mornings and Friday afternoons, says one school of thought, are not good times to attempt such calls. On the other hand, the opposing view is that such an assumption should not be made.

Keep a record of the time you began and the time you finished your telesales, and break up each hour into segments on your call record sheet. At the end of your selling day, check which hours were most successful, and whether your effectiveness tailed off at any point. Once you learn the maximum period for which you can be effective on the telephone, you will save the extra expense of making further calls that your experience tells you would be unproductive.

Telephone sales record			
Today's Date:		Start Time	
To mark the end of each hour's telephoning, skip two lines			
Company	Contact name	Telephone	Result
Assessment			
Number of: Calls	Contacts	Appointments	Success rate
Hour 1 Hour 2 Hour 3			

effective telephone techniques

The telephone can be used in tandem with a mailshot or as a stand-alone sales tool. Even in a non-sales situation, anyone who wishes to be in business should be aware of the techniques that will help to generate a successful image.

The first point worth remembering is that the voice, when heard through the medium of the telephone, is 20 to 30 times more expressive than when heard face to face. Perhaps this is because the voice is given the listener's full attention – you are right in their ear – without there being the distraction of a physical presence. Every nuance is detectable. They are automatically building up a 'picture' of you in their mind which will risk being blurred by the mixed messages that clothing and mannerisms can cause. This is why the voice is sometimes referred to as the 'second face'.

Perhaps this also explains, in part, the findings of one research project, namely that 73 per cent of businesspeople thought a business phone call more effective than a visit.

on the receiving end

To be thorough, let us first look at you as the receiver of a call:

- When you answer the telephone, a caller may be getting the first impression of your company, so be attentive and interested.
- Always keep a notepad and pen beside the phone.
- Answer the telephone immediately – it is sometimes company policy not to let a phone ring more than three times – and state your company name, your own name, and ask, 'May I help you?'
- Speak more slowly than you normally do.
- As in the case of a mailing, ask the caller to spell their name if necessary – they will be flattered more than insulted, and it is necessary to be certain.
- If you need to refer to files or otherwise delay the caller, refer back to them every 30 seconds to apologise for the delay.
- If it is clear that the enquiry cannot be dealt with quickly, suggest phoning them back, and do so as soon as possible.

- If the caller wishes to speak to someone else, ask, 'May I tell them who is calling, please?' Never 'Who is it?' or 'What's your name?'
- When you are advised of the caller's name, make the greeting personal: 'Good morning, Mrs Harvey. This is (your name). May I help you?'
- When taking a call for someone else, avoid saying, 'He'll call you back' if you can settle the query yourself.
- It is better not to take messages as these can be mislaid, garbled or forgotten. Take the caller's number, and arrange for him or her to be called back as soon as possible.
- You should not place your hand over the receiver while a caller is on the line, interrupt anyone who is in conversation with a caller or use catchphrases, clichés, jargon or slang.
- Be clear, definite, brief and precise.
- Callers must be made to feel that their call is a welcome event.
- Don't hold the telephone in the hand you need to make notes.

effective telephone technique can win over customers

With practice and the right techniques, the telephone can be the most cost-effective method for certain start-ups to reach and expand their market. The telephone introduction is a powerful and professional opening. It puts you in direct contact with each new prospect at minimum expense. It also puts the onus on that prospect to give you a fair and uninterrupted hearing.

You will be looking to obtain an order, or to arrange an appointment, the objective of which will be to obtain an order. Let us look at the techniques required.

preparation

Selling appointments over the telephone is a condensed and terse branch of the marketing function, and thorough preparation is vital. At all other stages of negotiation there will be room to correct errors or omissions. At this first stage you are either launched on course or stopped.

■ Set aside a time when you will not be disturbed.

■ Have your introduction written down and on the desk in front of you, with the objections you expect to meet and your reply to each. Use your own words, jargon free, along the lines suggested later on p 112.

■ Be sure your desk is tidy and in order, as this will aid your clarity of purpose.

■ Have a page listing the prospect company's name, type of business, name of contact and result of call. Phone in advance for the contact name if you need to.

■ If in any doubt as to who is the correct contact within a company, find out the managing director's name and ask to be put through to him or her. They will either deal with you themselves, or pass you to the person you should be speaking to. Having first gone to the top, you will be accorded more respect than if you had blundered from one official to the next, losing face.

■ Even if you do know the contact you should be speaking to, you could call the managing director beforehand to confirm that this is the correct contact. You can then begin your call to the contact by saying that the managing director said that you should talk to them.

■ Have your diary open and ready for entries.

■ Be in a courteous but firm frame of mind. This is a normal and acceptable business activity.

■ Read what you are going to say aloud to yourself a number of times before you begin the first call.

During the call, both your posture and your facial expression will convey themselves to the listener. If you are attentive and can express a smile, the listener will be more receptive to your suggestions.

You will need to control any nervousness and avoid repetition. Though it seems flippant, a little singing before you make a telephone call relaxes the vocal chords and improves voice quality.

Resist the urge to reveal more than you should. Your objective in using the telephone is to make an appointment – not to sell the product. Standing up to make the call can make you sound and feel more assertive, and moving about can help give expression to your voice as well as dissipating nervous energy. Interestingly, most women use their right ear to listen on the telephone and most men their left. The right hand side of the brain is said to control the empathic side of our nature, and this may be part of the reason why there are more women in tele-sales than men. Listening on the left-hand side of the brain taps into the logical side, useful for reasoned argument but not for empathy.

getting the green light

It is the job of switchboard operators and personal secretaries to vet each call as a matter of course. To get the green light straight through, you must keep the initiative.

In effect, this means that you do not allow any decisions to be made for you. Therefore, rather than asking the switchboard operator, 'May I speak with Mr Smith, please?', which is giving them power of veto, you might begin thus: 'Good afternoon. Is Mr Smith in?' If it is confirmed that he is, politely instruct the operator to put you through to him: 'Good! Put me through to him, please.'

When asked for your name, omit the title and give your first name: 'It's John, John Jones.' The double emphasis on your first name will help the operator to feel that Mr Smith knows you personally and would wish to speak with you.

Should you be switched through to the personal secretary, he or she may press to know the purpose of your call. Refer to a letter or direct mailshot if one has been sent. Otherwise say politely, 'It's a business matter. Could you put me through, please?'

There will be cases, usually in larger companies, where an executive's secretary has the authority to arrange their boss's appointments. They will volunteer the information if this is so.

If you are told that the prospect is busy:

■ Politely decline any offer that they should call you – this would be allowing the initiative to be taken away from you.

■ Ask at what time you should call back – this obliges the personal assistant to allow you access next time, since it was she who gave you the best time to call.

■ Make an entry in your diary for this to be done.

■ Keep to the agreement.

■ If the prospect is still not there, or is unavailable, tell the personal assistant that you have made an appointment to call on the prospect and give a date.

■ Write a letter to the prospect confirming this date.

This is a form of inertia selling, because you rely on the inertia of the prospect to allow the appointment to happen rather than going to the trouble of trying to change it. As long as the company is on your route, you will not waste much time by calling in. Your letter confirming your appointment will give you credence. You also have the name of the personal assistant to refer to. Phone on the day before such an inertia appointment. You then have a stronger opening than you did at the outset. You are calling to confirm an appointment as opposed to asking for one.

you're through now

When you are put through to your prospect, they will have two questions uppermost in their mind:

■ Who is this on the telephone?
■ What is the purpose of their call?

You must first give a verbal handshake and then immediately answer these two questions. For example: 'Good afternoon, Mr Smith. My name is John Jones of Star Security Systems. I am phoning to arrange an appointment with you to demonstrate how our latest electronic alarm particularly suits your company.'

Brevity is the essence of success over the telephone. You are selling the sizzle, not the steak. Now that he knows what he needs to know, close. For example: 'We'll be visiting firms in your area during the week ending the 27th. Would you prefer Wednesday the 23rd or Friday the 25th?' This means of closing is effective because it is offering alternatives, either of which presupposes consent. Once you have put the question, wait for the prospect to answer. If there is a pause, wait for him or her to fill it.

resolving objections

Should prospects put forward any objection, then they are conversing with you, which is good. They need your help to make up their minds. Take care not to seem to be pouncing back with your reply, nor to sound glib or argumentative. Tact is the ability to make a point without making an enemy, as the adage puts it.

Remember the objective of your call – an appointment – and ask for this as you unravel each objection.

Here are three of the most usual objections, each followed with a suitable response:

'Why can't you tell me about it now?'

'I'd like to, Mr Smith, but it would take more of your time to explain it to you now than it would in person, which is why it is better to meet. Would you prefer Wednesday the 23rd or Friday the 25th?'

'Send me literature.'

'I'll certainly be glad to do that – it will help you to prepare questions which I'll be happy to answer when we meet. Would you prefer Wednesday the 23rd or Friday the 25th, Mr Smith?'

'I'm sorry, but I'm too busy to meet you.'

'I realise that you are very busy, Mr Smith, and that is why I'm phoning in advance to arrange an appointment that fits in with your schedule. Would you prefer Wednesday the 23rd or Friday the 25th?'

You may find that suggesting a meeting before or after normal business hours fits in better with your prospect's plans. It could even be that your product will save time, which will be a strong incentive for them to meet you.

You can also parry objections, or redirect a conversation, with the use of what is known as 'leading' questions that will elicit a positive response. These will take the form of factual statements, followed by a request that can be confirmed, which has the effect of your prospect agreeing with you.

It could be said that you are collecting an armful of positive responses to put your prospect in an agreeable state of mind. You will also be affirming in their mind that you have a clear vision of who they are as a company, and they will be more curious to know how your product will fit in:

'Your company is a road haulage contractor, isn't it, Mr Brown?'

'And you are the Transport Manager, aren't you, Mr Brown?'

'You are interested in keeping costs to a minimum, aren't you, Mr Brown?'

'Then I am certain that you will be interested in what I can show you. Would you prefer Wednesday the 23rd or Friday the 25th?'

fixing the time and finishing

Once they have chosen a date, they must then choose a time. An appointment set on the hour suggests that you will keep them for a full hour. An appointment set at half past the hour suggests that you'll keep them at least half an hour.

Fixing an appointment at ten minutes before each hour helps to instil a feeling that the meeting can be wrapped up quite quickly, if need be. Again, give a choice:

'Would you prefer 8.50 am or 3.50 pm, Mr Brown?'

With the day and time of the appointment now set, give your thanks, say that you will confirm the appointment in writing, bid your goodbye and put down the receiver. Enter into no further conversation.

In the results column of your prospect list, record the outcome of your call. Record any information that will help you to personalise future contact as well. You have begun a relationship, and this should always be developing.

evaluation

Take a moment to evaluate your performance so as to pinpoint and remove any weakness and renew your resolve. You can record your telesales conversations. Whether or not you do, ask yourself how you felt you handled the call. Be totally honest with yourself.

Although you may have gone through your introduction a dozen times in this one sitting, your next prospect has not heard it from you before.

Move towards your next call as if it were the only call you had to make today. Turn the full beam of your attention on each new prospect, and make them feel that it is just them you are interested in. Be friendly and professional in your manner and your prospects will feel that they are being given preferential treatment.

Telephone selling of this sort, where it can be used, ensures a cost-effective sales effort by isolating those companies that are prepared to allot time to consider your product at minimum outlay. It also enables you to obtain useful and correct information for your records, which will help you to bond with your prospects in the future, and expand your sales to them because of your knowledge of their needs.

Those prospects who will not meet you can be assessed either as likely candidates for a second call in the future, or as definitely not worth a second attempt. Even this information is useful in that you will never need to spend more time or money on those companies you are sure will not use you.

One of the factors that must be quickly faced up to in a tele-sales situation is the high incidence of calls that find the prospect unavailable. One estimate has it that only once in every seven calls you make will you end up catching and speaking to the person you want.

Since it is usually the managing director, or other such high-ranking individual, you wish to speak to, this should come as no surprise. Such a person will have a schedule that will often mean being away from the office or involved in meetings. The advantage to you in the medium term is that when you are the person in the meeting with the managing director, it is just as likely that you will be given that undivided attention.

At the end of each tele-sales session, work out:

1. the total number of calls you have made;
2. the total number of prospects you have spoken to directly;
3. the total number of appointments you have won.

To establish your hit rate, divide 2 by 3. If you have made 25 calls, spoken directly with 12 prospects, and made two appointments, your hit rate is one in six.

You will be encouraged to find that, with practice, this hit rate gets better and better. This means that your technique is improving and that each appointment is costing you less to make. From my own personal experience of making sales appointments over the telephone, an average of two appointments for every five contacts made is achievable.

Once you detect this regular pattern in your work, it acts as a motivator. If you have made five calls without winning an appointment, you sit back and change up a gear. You know from experience that you have to, and will, get those appointments.

Remember, there are a variety of telephone line providers in the marketplace now, creating a competitive market of which you can take advantage.

preparing for sales visits

You will need to attune your presentation to suit the culture of the company you'll be visiting. You will already have done some preliminary research before you made the telesales call to secure the appointment. You will now need to build and expand on that. If the firm is reasonably large, you could:

■ read the company's literature and advertisements to get a feel for their attitudes;
■ find out if there is a cyclical system of buying which you would need to be aware of in order to time your sales pitch most effectively;
■ order a copy of their yearly accounts from Companies House;
■ ask others who have dealt with them about their experience of the prospect company;
■ read the company's recruitment ads – these are a good guide to the corporate values of an organisation.

Since success equals the setting up and achieving of goals, refer to the sales targets you put in the business plan, and monitor your progress to make certain that you stay on course. On the basis of your achievements you may need to recast your projections in the business plan, and analyse the effect this has.

Each day that has been set aside for selling must be structured so as to minimise rush and uncertainty. Adequate time slots must be allowed for each visit, each journey between, and a midday break to eat and to relax.

a clear focus

Before the milk hits the cornflakes, you must be clearly focused on the objective of each appointment, be it to protect turnover from competition, develop an existing account or to open a new account.

You must be clear:

■ how your product can be used beneficially by the customer or prospect;
■ how your competitors compare with you;
■ how your customer or prospect runs their business;
■ how new trends in the marketplace might affect your offer or your customer's attitude to it.

You will do best to group appointments in the same area. This means careful route-planning to save time, money and energy.

Especially in the case of a new account, you will need to have prepared a script using your own words, without jargon or cant, describing your product. Couch this in terms of what it does for the buyer rather than what it is.

As with a mailshot, use the phrase 'which means that' to translate features into benefits. For example: 'It is made from aluminium, which means that it will not rust, so it is a once-only cost.'

So that the buyer can distil the exact meaning from your words, it is important to be brief and relevant. By enlarging beyond what is effective, you will be obscuring your point by hiding it among subsidiary facts.

Avoid the tendency to alter your script during its delivery, except perhaps when buyers are ready to commit themselves and further illustration becomes superfluous.

Since the buyer sees you briefly and seldom, you must use the opportunity to appear neat, clean and well organised. This will reflect attention to detail and pride in maintaining high standards. It is better to have abstained from garlic, or anything that will carry on the breath – except, of course, when travelling through Transylvania.

When you arrive at your appointment, treat everyone with courtesy. The receptionist could be a relative of the managing director. If your name is to be phoned through, offer your business card so that your details are passed on correctly. Be relaxed and comfortable to be with.

ways to make the buyers buy

Assertiveness rather than aggressiveness or accommodating behaviour is an asset in gaining the respect you will require from the buyer. This means that, should you be met in the reception area or waiting room, for example, and asked to make your presentation there, you should not succumb to these conditions but should suggest instead that you adjourn to the buyer's office.

It also means that you should not create adverse conditions for yourself by using such expressions as 'I was just passing' or 'I wonder if you could spare me a few minutes of your time?', as you will be lowering yourself in their estimation.

delivery impact

You must take care, too, that your handshake is neither too weak nor too strong. A moderately firm clasp is ideal, accompanied by an unforced smile.

The very first thing you will need to sell to any buyer is yourself. You have to be liked and trusted. Being liked is just the natural concomitant to liking others, so see the buyer as a person first, and relate to him or her on an equal footing. The buyer is a potential customer, and customers are a part of your business – not outsiders.

Cover the initial few minutes with small talk about the weather, or a compliment relevant to the buyer's premises, or a query as to whether he or she received your letter confirming the appointment, or anything neutral and unprovocative. Once you are in the buyer's office, wait to be asked to sit down before you do so.

Seating positions help to create or ease tensions. Face-to-face is confrontational. Side by side does not aid communication, but can be used by allies who are already accustomed to one another. The right-angled position is best, as this allows easy, unforced eye contact.

Having carefully prepared your script, you will now deliver it in such a way as to convey its import clearly. If your voice sounds enthusiastic and firm, this will prove infectious.

At the end of your explanation, keep quiet and let the buyer talk. Listen supportively again, keeping eye contact and using reflective and open-ended questions when required to swell his flow.

If you listen carefully, you'll be told what the buyer's needs are. Match the benefits of your product to their needs and you'll create the desire to buy.

objections are to be expected, and are useful

It is natural for a buyer to look for any problems in advance. As with telesales, a pattern of objections will emerge, some of which you had anticipated, others of which will be new to you.

The best way to deal with objections, as you learn what they are, is to build them into your introduction, and explain them away in advance. For example, if you are selling vehicle signage, a buyer might object that by putting signs on his or her vehicles he is reducing their resale value because they will have to be resprayed by the next owner. However, your signs might well be the self-adhesive vinyl sort, not traditionally painted on. Therefore, this objection can be dealt with in your introduction thus: 'This system of vehicle signage can be removed should you wish to sell the vehicle, which means that its resale value will not be adversely affected.'

Any objections that do arise will be useful in that:

- They indicate the distance yet to be covered.
- They keep communication lines open.
- They may uncover a need you had not been aware of.
- They may bring to light any misunderstanding on the buyer's part, which you now have the chance to put right.
- You will be better prepared for this objection hereafter.
- Part of knowing your product or service is knowing all the reasons why someone might *not* want to buy it.
- When it is done well, people actually like being sold to – even more, they expect to be! Offering objections can often, in part, be a way of extending the pleasure of making a purchase.

Take the attitude that you are being asked for a clearer view of how your offer relates to the buyer. In a way, they are saying, 'I would like to buy this product, but there are a few points I'd like you to clear up first.' Therefore, listen supportively, avoid pouncing or snapping back with a reply as this will give the impression that instead of listening carefully, you've just been waiting for your turn to speak.

Mirror the buyer's body language, as this will help to create empathy between you. Reflect the buyer's questions back, if you want him or her to be more specific. For example: 'So you think that red and yellow might be too bright?'

To mellow the effect of what might appear to be any objections the buyer has, use empathic phrasing such as 'I'm glad you've made that point' or 'I understand exactly what you are saying' as a preface to your reply.

Avoid using jargon or technical terms, unless you are with the initiated. Answer each objection without any trace of antagonism, and with a welcoming attitude that invites their interest.

If, ultimately, you feel that objections have persisted beyond what would seem to be reasonable, it is likely that the objections are a cover for the real reason: the buyer is non-committal. Stop, and use what is called the 'list back' technique. You list each objection the buyer has made, and read them back, pointing out that you have answered each one, and ticking them off as you go through them. At the end of the list, pause for a moment to read it over in silence to yourself. Then look up and say: '... and the other reason is?' This should elicit the real reason that is bothering the buyer. It might be a matter of pride: until now, the buyer has been unable to admit that your product is beyond his or her budget. Your solution to this might be that the total can be reached by instalments.

When, however, you are at the end of your presentation but find that the sale is not closing itself, then the onus is on you to close it. Some methods of doing this are:

- *Direct close*: where you ask directly for the order.
- *Alternative close*: 'Would you like the black one or the gold one?' or, 'Shall I start next Monday or the Monday afterwards?'
- *Assumption close*: 'Very good then. You will receive delivery before the weekend.'
- *The conditional close*: he or she asks, 'Could you deliver within a week of ordering?' You reply, 'If I could, would you buy now?'
- *Reference close*: a personal reference for your product from someone whom the buyer would have knowledge of, in a similar business to theirs.
- *The caution or fear close*: a list of the buyer's competitors who are using what you are offering to their advantage – possibly leaving the buyer's company less competitive. At time of writing, one of the major mortgage lenders is using this motivator on a poster selling insurance: there is a photograph of a family with the father blanked out in white and a caption urging the reader to consider what would happen to the family if the worst should happen.

■ *The free trial or puppy dog close*: lend someone a puppy for a week and they will want to keep it. A free trial of your product may have the same effect. It will also switch the emphasis from your having to explain why the buyer should use you, to the buyer's having to explain why he or she doesn't need to.

■ *The concession close*: this should be used with discretion, and probably only when you have been having buying signals, which need a nudge of this sort to bring them into the open. However, without the buyer already being interested, concessions would only serve to lower you in his or her esteem.

Once you have asked for a commitment, stop and wait. Resist the temptation to fill the void. The buyer may be running through your offer in their mind and your interference may be unwelcome, and jeopardise a favourable outcome. If the buyer asks a question, answer briefly.

having closed, leave

It is quite likely that you will have made a sale, given that you targeted the right sort of company, had your objectives and how to attain them clear in your mind, and kept to professional guidelines. Once you have made the sale, anything else you say about it can only work against you. Switch the subject away, and completely avoid such comments as 'You've made the right decision' or 'You'll be glad you bought this.'

Since the buyer has seen fit to buy your product, you should ask for the names of others that they feel might be interested in your offer, and give the buyer a pen and paper to write them down as they think of them.

Be sure to leave two business cards, one for the buyer and one that the buyer can pass on to those among his or her contacts who might ask for your details.

Make your valedictory remarks, keeping them brief, pleasant and unself-centred. Shake hands, thank the buyer and promptly leave.

Once back in your car, write a summary of your visit on the relevant file, while the details are still fresh in your mind. As is advisable in most post-sales situations, ask yourself whether you did as well as you could. This judgement does not need to be based on whether you obtained the buyer's commitment. You might have performed perfectly and not obtained a sale, but have the satisfaction of being certain that there was not a sale to be had in this instance.

Spend a few moments re-running the sales interview, and iron out the imperfections in your mind so as to reduce the likelihood of their occurring at your next appointment.

This done, scan the file that refers to the next visit you will be making that day to refresh your memory, then turn the full beam of your attention towards the task in hand.

the end of the selling week

At the end of each week, work out the cost of your visits to be set against the profit you made from your sales.

If you made 50 telephone calls, out of which you spoke to 25 prospects, four of whom agreed to an appointment, and two of whom made a positive buying decision as a result of that appointment, have your costs all been covered? Have you made a profit? If not, then you should be able to work out how many extra telesales calls you need to make to create the extra appointments which will bring you the extra sales needed to push you into profit.

You are your own sales manager, and careful forward planning of your appointment schedule should ensure that travelling expenses are controlled, and time is used effectively. The better your journeys are organised, with a minimum of travelling time between each appointment, the more appointments you can make for that day. This will increase the time available for selling. Selling should increase sales, and sales will increase income and the likelihood of profit.

The time you allow for each sales appointment should relate directly to the importance of the account to your business. If it is the local newsagent you are seeing, he will only be able to place a modest order with you. If it is the buyer from Woolworths, she can have a major effect, and must be dealt with in more detail.

So you must strive to achieve visits that are within easy distance of one another, and you must adjust the time of each visit to fit in that extra hour of selling such a strategy can clear space for. If you spend three days a week selling, this will mean an extra three hours per week, more than 12 hours per month extra selling time. Your end-of-year accounts will show the positive effect of this.

Other ways to trim any waste from your selling day are:

■ Make appointments for before and after normal working hours, as these are the times when the day's hectic phase has passed, and managers will often have more time to give you.

■ If an appointment finishes earlier than expected, ring ahead to your next appointment and bring it forward.

■ If the next appointment cannot be brought forward, use the time you now have to either make cold calls on other local businesses, or begin making appointments by phone for the following week.

development of existing accounts

You will quickly begin to build up a database of prospects, some of whom will be customers, some of whom will remain prospects a while longer, and some of whom you will not be destined to do business with.

■ Twenty per cent of your customers will give you 80 per cent of your turnover. It is clearly in your interest to identify and cultivate this 20 per cent.

■ Try to switch your regulars to an annual contract or to a monthly retainer, thus bonding their custom in a way your bank manager will appreciate.

■ Localise and reduce transactions that are non-profit making.

■ The majority of your existing customers will be happy to supply you with referrals, which is the soundest route to new business.

■ Since 20 per cent of your customers will fall away each year, you should vet your list carefully to pinpoint those who might be so inclined. Remedial action can then be taken.

your company image

Your company image is created by every item and action used to promote it. Your telephone manner, your appearance, the quality and design of your letterheads and business cards, the wording on mailshots and on company vehicles all go towards forming a distinct impression in the eye of the potential or established customer.

Image is the projection of the company's personality. It can convey what you would like the company to be. Although it is conceptual, it is not cosmetic.

If you look at many shop doors you will see signs that read bluntly 'No Dogs Allowed'. If you look at the entrance to a Marks and Spencer store, on the other hand, the sign will probably say something like 'Guide Dogs Only'. This is an indication of distinctive corporate values in action. Every signal given out by a company helps to build or destroy trust; helps to welcome or deter a customer; helps to make buying easy.

In one survey of 450 UK companies, it was found that the larger a company became, the more difficult it was to translate corporate values into action. Sixty-four per cent of small companies said that they were proud of the way they treated customers against only 45 per cent in larger companies.

In the same survey, 82 per cent of the companies agreed that properly implemented corporate values contribute to profitability. This means that you will be well advised to spend as much time as necessary getting the values central to your company's thinking clarified and translated into a definite visual message or identity.

How you go about this will differ to some degree in each case. Some new companies, for example, that wish to project a solid, established image will sometimes use the ploy of registering for VAT, even though they have not reached the necessary earnings threshold. This goes back to the point made in the early part of Chapter 1 – projecting forward to a desired change and behaving as if it has already happened.

Their prospects and customers will then assume that their turnover is greater than it really is, which makes them seem more successful than they really are. To the companies that choose to do this, the extra administration that being registered for VAT involves is well worth the effort in terms of the boost it gives their company image.

Your company image should reflect your business and the standard of product and service it provides, and be directly geared to suit the markets at which your business is targeted. Knowing your company's strengths and the direction it will take, you must breathe life into this identity by meaningful use of design, colour and presentation. The importance of this as part of your marketing activity can best be illustrated by analogy: would you feel confident if an aeroplane taking you abroad was dirty, with peeling paint and a pilot who was unkempt?

For livery, letterheads, logos and business cards, the buffs, beiges, creams, mushrooms, creamy browns and the olive greens all give out an impression of understated quality and quiet confidence.

The quality of the paper used for your letterheads can give added value to your company too. A good printer can show you the wide selection of colours and quality available and their costs. The larger the batch you buy, the cheaper per page it will be. A combination of colours in your logo can more easily project an image of prosperity and confidence.

The colours of your suit, tie, shirt, socks, briefcase and company car also help create the overall picture of your company in the mind of the buyer.

Even if what you intend to do does not entail wearing a suit, the same thinking carries across. Look clean and presentable. If there are more than one of you, select overalls, uniforms or suits of the same colour and style. Toolboxes could carry the company logo and slogan, if applicable.

Always be on the look-out for ways in which you can put your company a shade or more ahead of the competition. For example, if you need public liability insurance, the difference in cost to you of obtaining £500,000 worth and £1 million worth is minor. The difference in a customer's perception of your company when they hear that key £1 million figure mentioned is major.

Or, if you are asked the same questions by each customer after each job is finished or product sold, why not have the answers printed on a card or letterhead, with a thank-you to the customer included? If, for example, you are a plasterer, these questions might be:

■ How long will it take for the plaster to dry?
■ How soon can I start decorating?

Your leaflet, which could incorporate your logo and the insignia of any trade organisation you are a member of, could read:

Under normal indoor drying conditions, modern lightweight plasters will dry out within four days. You can tell that the process is finished when the colour has changed from being dark to being very light. It is important that no artificial heat should be used to shorten the drying out period, or the setting process will be affected.

Once these four days have elapsed, you may either paper or paint the new surface by following these guidelines:

1. If papering, coat the surface with a product called 'size'.
2. If painting, coat the surface with an alkaline-based primer or, in the absence of this, with a PVA-based primer such as Unibond or Feb Bond. There are a number of different brands on the market.

Thank you for doing business with our company. We hope that everything has been to your satisfaction.

This will add that final fillip to the job you have done, and is a step above answering the customers' questions verbally. They will be both surprised and pleased at your professionalism. You will be one step ahead of the competition.

As a final touch, it will seal the good impression you should have created from the first moment you were seen by the customer through the execution of the work, on to the moment when you made sure you left everywhere as clean as possible.

Another marketing opportunity still much underused is the blank space on the back of business cards. Why not have a promotional paragraph or two printed here, explaining your company's product, and how it fills customers' needs? Or use the space for two or three brief quotes from satisfied customers?

Or you could use the space to state your terms of business, followed by a smaller promotional piece. For example:

Please note that payments should be made in cash unless otherwise agreed. This is due to the time it takes for cheques to clear.

This company is insured for public liability up to £1 million and is a member of the Chamber of Trade, Commerce and Industry.

A company that sells kitchens could present the lady of the house with a bouquet of flowers once the job is complete. Although this device in particular would not carry across to every situation, going that extra mile does help to cement the feel-good factor in the customer's mind. The flowers will make the kitchen look even nicer too!

These flourishes are not directly connected with the selling act, since the sale has already been made. They are part of the broader marketing activity that helps to establish trust and an enjoyment in having been associated with you in the mind of the buyer or customer. They will also help to earn you that best of all selling devices, the personal recommendation. In the case of repeat business too, your customer will only return to you if they have been wholeheartedly impressed. Try to develop a mindset where you 'underpromise and overdeliver', rather than the reverse.

customer care

Your customers are your most valuable asset as a business. You have managed to obtain their commitment in the form of a sale to them but, because there is sometimes little to choose between suppliers, you will need to court their favour continuously.

Customer care can be most readily seen in the levels of reliability and service you offer both before and after a sale. Keeping to deadlines should be part of your company ethos and be seen as an opportunity to build trust between your business and the customer whom it serves.

Once the product transaction is complete, you should think of ways in which you can maintain the good relationship you have begun with the customer. These might include:

- keeping your customers informed of special offers of which they might wish to take advantage;
- a telephone call or postcard to inform your customer that a service is now due;
- a courtesy call three months after the transaction to be sure of their satisfaction;
- an offer to put right any genuine defect;

- ■ a prompt response to such a request;
- ■ a discount on their next purchase;
- ■ an invitation to a special event;
- ■ a guarantee.

And now a bracing thought: 'It is an immutable law in business that words are words, explanations are explanations, promises are promises – but only performance is reality.' Harold Geneen, former chief executive, International Telegraph and Telephone Co.

the Internet

Using the Internet Smarter and Faster by Brooke Broadbent (which is also published by Kogan Page as part of the *Sunday Times* Creating Success series) goes into the depth this subject deserves, but for our present purposes a brief overview will suffice.

The first thing to say is that in general the law applies to activities on the Internet in the same way as it applies to non-Internet activity. In short, if something is illegal offline it is likely to be illegal online as well. That aside, the Internet, or 'Net', is a powerfully useful tool that enables you not just to research your business's potential, but to refer to useful statistics, to obtain information about your competitors, to winkle out what sources of practical and financial assistance might be available for start-ups, and to ask for and obtain specific advice tailored to your circumstances. You can even obtain route directions between two points, train and bus timetables, or book accommodation or flights online. You could of course have your own Web page to advertise what you do, receive enquiries and even accept orders.

The value of the Internet, in both our private and our business lives, is difficult to overestimate. It is already being said that the Internet is set to have a greater impact on business than did the fax and even the telephone and, once you see its worth, that is difficult to argue with. Aside from anything else, electronic mail (e-mail) is probably the most efficient and certainly the speediest form of communication of all. It travels at 7,000 miles per second. You'll wonder how you ever did without it.

Connecting to the Internet is becoming simpler because service providers are competing with one another to win business. Even if you don't have the wherewithal to link up directly, most local libraries provide free Internet access to the public.

managing the business

You are now your own boss, or intend to be. This means learning how to give yourself orders, which in turn means organisation. In real terms the smooth running of your business will come from planning.

Naturally, you will have an overall plan for the year, based on achieving certain targets. This has to be broken down into monthly and then weekly components of the plan, forming a clear strategy by which the plan will be fulfilled. Each part of this strategy must be reviewed at its end, and its achievements measured against its targets. This will allow for any necessary shifts in policy, should there be clear shortfalls or should demand exceed expectations.

If you are fortunate enough to have an employee or partner to whom you can delegate, then clearly an element of your work can be dealt with in this way.

managing your time

From the start, you will need to diarise any holidays, special occasions, trade shows and so on, so that you can plan around them.

You are aware from your business plan what level of sales you need to achieve. You will quickly learn how much effort and time this will take.

Sales are a front-line activity. For a start-up business in particular, the front line should be defended and dealt with before going behind the lines to attend to any resulting administration, bookkeeping, production, and so on.

Diarise the time you need each week to:

■ make sales appointments;
■ attend sales appointments;
■ service sales made.

Your diary will now show you how much time you have left. For a start-up business, this will not just be the nine-to-five slots. It is very likely that you will need to use evenings and weekends whenever necessary.

One straightforward way to clear the demands on your time is to list the week's tasks according to their order of importance, under three headings:

1. Must be done
2. Should be done
3. Would like to do

Use a ruled copybook and pencil (so you can make changes) to keep a record. This could be either hard-backed for durability or pocket-sized for portability.

Once you read the breakdown under each heading, it may become clear that some of the tasks deserve a higher or lower rating, so change them. Estimate the time each will take. What others perceive as urgent may not be urgent in your case. If at all in doubt, list the item in the second or third column, and look at it again a day or two on. Its apparent urgency will have disappeared or increased by then.

Examples that might come under each heading include:

1. *Must be done* would have to include those tasks that can only be performed during normal office hours, and that have a direct effect on your turnover.

2. *Should be done* might include a telephone call to arrange an appointment with your lender to increase your overdraft.

3. *Would like to do* could include attending a meeting of the local business club for a presentation and to make contacts or 'network'. This very useful activity enables you to link up with other small businesses, to help one another or to pass on jobs you cannot do yourself.

The reason for keeping a record of this exercise is so that at each week's end you can review your progress and adjust the coming week's lists to reflect changed or new priorities. That appointment with your lender might now be imperative or, better than that, unnecessary, and so would occupy a new slot.

This simple form of management by objectives can itself be broken down further, to ensure that your time is being put to optimum use. Carry the list with you during the day. As you complete each task, tick it off and write in the actual time it took. At the end of the day's work, check the difference between the estimated time and the actual time taken, and write this alongside. The exercise will show you where you are spending too much time for the return given, and will offer you the chance of trimming the time you have allowed for that task. Or it may be that the task *must* be done and so your estimated time may have to be adjusted upwards. At the end of each week, each month and each year you can work out where your efforts have been put.

The time spent in making this record is more than justified. By being able to see clearly where your time goes, you will easily detect areas for improvement.

'making' time

There are ways to fit even more into your business day, which achieves the effect of making time.

■ We tend to fill the time we have allocated for a task, whether or not that task really needs that time.

■ Cut down the estimated time for each task so that you do it in half or three-quarters of the time.

■ In the morning, condition yourself to getting out of bed at the time you should, rather than taking another 40 winks. A few minutes to orientate and focus your mind is good, but any more is wasteful. Since you have to get up, get up.

■ You know that the post office or bank will be more likely to have a queue at certain times of the week, so choose other times when you can just dart in and out.

■ 'Home banking' might tie in better with your busy schedule. Should your bank offer this service, it is a simple matter to arrange, and gives you access to your account 24 hours a day, using your telephone or the 'net'.

■ You know that the roads will be blocked by traffic during the rush hours, so arrange your schedule to skirt around these times.

■ On longer journeys, taking a train will mean being able to use that time to deal with administration. Book that train well ahead – it should cost you less.

■ Many of us spend an average of 20 hours a week watching television. This is a leisure activity that you should allow yourself in smaller portions, perhaps as a reward for meeting certain goals.

Refer to your copybook list and diary and, if you are falling behind, increase your pace. This can be done by:

■ Making non-sales phone calls briefer. (Sales calls should already be of a set length.) This means mentioning at the beginning of the conversation that you are going to be brief, and having your points written down in front of you.

■ If small talk is necessary, leave it until the end of the call, and deal with your points first.

■ Some calls will not require a conversation with the person involved, so leave a detailed message and take the name of the person to whom you give it. Write this down.

■ A fax would accomplish the same purpose.

■ Some phone calls or faxes can be couched in such a way as to require an answer only if the party disagrees.

■ Those phone calls which you know you can be quickest with, leave to the end of your list. You could then speed them up further if necessary.

■ Drop a note instead of a letter and, unless typing is essential, handwrite it.

■ Use text messages or e-mail.

Part of your schedule should have included time for the unforeseen, those interruptions or minor emergencies that are part and parcel of a day's routine. Human nature will sometimes use this unforeseen element as a means of escaping the responsibilities to hand, so avoid spending more time on interruptions than you need to.

Deal with interruptions by deflection, explaining that you are busy but pencilling each item on tomorrow's page, which you will be breaking down into its three columns that evening. In this way you will have freed your mind and know that the matter will be dealt with in its place. This also has the advantage of returning the initiative to you.

There is no need to pencil in the matter to be dealt with at a future date if you know in your heart that you would really just like to say 'no'. Learn to say 'no' to situations that require it. There is no need to be blunt. You can take the sting out of your 'no' by wrapping it in an 'If only I had known beforehand' or 'Really, I'd like to, but...'

If you have to go to the town centre, wait until there is more than one reason for going. Perhaps there will be some visits you could make on the way, or while there, that would make fuller use of that time.

shortening meetings

A good means of shortening any meetings which you find by experience take too long, is to hold them while standing up. People will be much more to the point and you will find the necessary allotment of time more than halved.

Otherwise, state the time you have available, state the agenda, and state that one must fit the other. Meetings held before lunch or late afternoon tend to be short, as people want to dash off. Sometimes a meeting will drag on because neither party brings it to a specific conclusion. It is not impolite to help the meeting to an end with such a simple remark as 'Well, I think we've covered everything now.'

the early bird

Perhaps one of the simplest ways of making time is to get up early in the morning before the world starts getting noisy – 6 am is good – when there will be no chance of an interruption. Your mind should be at its clearest; you will produce more because you are fresh; you will feel on top of things because you are ahead of most people already, and because you will have mapped out today's priorities using the 'must, should and like to' formula.

If you are a person who does not find that morning is their strongest time, watch your work habits and see when you produce best. Leave important tasks that need a clear head until this time.

Have your work area tidy and ready for take-off from the previous evening. Have everything you need in place and ready for you. Otherwise, you might find an excuse to delay action.

There is a saying that action speaks louder than words. There is another, more pointed saying, however, that action is not necessarily progress.

Everything that isn't indispensable is useless. Keep your goals in mind and trim your activities and tasks down to those that bring you that much nearer to achieving them within their timetable. That's progress. Most pointedly, long hours of themselves do not mean anything. Results count, not effort.

managing your cash flow

The cash flow projections made in your business plan will have allowed you adequate time to build in protection against the possible shortage of working capital in your business. As already suggested, however, these projections will need to be compared to actual cashflow on a regular basis. The difference can then be imposed upon the business plan projections, the effect analysed and the altered situation dealt with.

Another good monitoring method is to keep close tally of the number of quotations, proposals or estimates your business puts out each month, and the percentage of acceptances. Any fluctuation in this number pattern might signal a change in your fortunes. Likewise, the ratio that each individual expense represents against sales should be kept track of, as this might indicate the need to increase sales or the price you charge your customers.

If you meet your sales targets and are paid on completion of each job or project, and you keep within your projected outgoings, you are unlikely to meet with a cash flow problem. Most businesses are obliged to give credit, however, and thus must incorporate credit management systems to keep accounts up to date, and ensure that working capital does not dry up.

A deposit against the order may be possible. In some trades, this may be agreed to cover the cost of materials.

In other instances, such as when a customer is exceeding their credit limit, is uncreditworthy, or is new on your books, you could issue a pro forma invoice requesting a deposit or perhaps even the entire amount.

■ Check that the client is creditworthy. This might involve checking the company's latest accounts at

Companies House, contacting one of the credit reference agencies, getting the advice of a solicitor who offers credit referencing, asking for bank references or asking among the company's known suppliers.

■ Check on the age of a company; less than three years is considered to be very young, with staying power still in question.

■ Set a credit limit for each customer and do not allow this to be exceeded.

■ Send out bills and invoices promptly – issue them on-site upon completion if practicable.

■ Build in a very closely monitored system listing monies owed, by whom, for how long.

■ Start with those whose debt is outstanding longest. Phone them. If they say they are sending a cheque, ask them to fax a copy of this over immediately – this will help to flush out the ingenuous. Alternatively, ask for the cheque number. At your discretion, warn that no further supplies will be issued, or that you will sue. Charge interest on overdue accounts.

■ Always ask for credit for your own company.

■ Keep stock levels related to sales.

■ Meticulous record-keeping, particularly where big companies are concerned, is of the essence. You will need to keep original estimates, dates of previous invoices, precise times and dates of any phone calls, and names of those to whom you have already spoken.

■ In some instances, it may be possible to factor your debtors, obtaining an advance of up to 80 per cent against these. Factoring and financial discounting are financial services designed to improve the cash flow of healthy, growing companies, and as such may not be available to you in the first or introductory stage of growth.

■ Otherwise, you could hand responsibility for the collection of your debts to a debt-collecting firm, or the debt recovery department of a firm of solicitors.

Taking someone to court is a costly procedure in terms of time and administration, so this option must be weighed against the amount owed, and a considered judgement made as to whether this final action is worthwhile.

Check firms of solicitors for what is called a 'pre-action service'. This is a service whereby the solicitors will send a letter requesting payment, followed by a telephone call to find out why payment is being delayed, if it still is, followed by a report to you on what action to take next if no result has been obtained. This 'pre-action service' sometimes entails no cost to you, and is a good preliminary to going to court. The service is best used in the early stages of a debt problem when its success rate is high. This success rate deteriorates for debts that have existed for a year or more.

If you choose to supply goods on a 'sale or return' basis, restrict this facility to your best customers only, and if the goods are not sold quickly enough, nor in sufficient quantity, consider withdrawing the facility. As emphasised previously, you are in business to make a profit, and this is not helped by maintaining stocks that remain unsold on someone else's premises.

To discourage your customers from using you as a credit facility, you could use a two-tier pricing system where the full price is charged for those on credit, but discounts are given to those who pay on delivery or completion. This could also be used to encourage a customer to buy in quantity, and most will expect to be offered this as an option.

Make it easy for your customer to pay by offering as many means of payment as you can in your circumstances. Anything that encourages customers to buy, or makes it easier for them, is likely to mean extra sales.

Can you arrange to accept payment by cash, cheque or credit card? Cheques would need to be backed by a cheque guarantee card, or allowed to clear before despatch of goods, and you would need to negotiate an arrangement with the credit card companies, which take a commission on each sale in which their cards are used.

This kind of information can be printed as part of your advertising literature, in your advertisements, or on a standard order form included as part of your advertising, along with such information as whether orders can be taken by telephone, fax or letter.

Though late payment legislation seems a good idea at first airing, there is a current opinion that believes that this will not alter the balance of power between large and small firms. Such legislation may only result in dominant customers insisting on extended credit terms, leaving small firms to wait even longer. Indeed, in the North West one survey showed that only 1 per cent of the business community believe that late payment is due to the absence of legislation. A tighter focus on credit terms and credit control will have the best effect at grass roots level.

employing people

If you decide you need to take on paid help, it is worth spending time and trouble to get the right person, as much of your success will depend on them. The Inland Revenue have useful leaflets on employing people; see their Web site, www. inlandrevenue.gov.uk, or ring their Helpline for the Newly Self-Employed, 08459 154515.

If you advertise the position, be careful not to express or imply that the vacancy is open only to one sex, one race or only to people of a particular marital status. This carries through to the selection procedure, where it is unlawful to discriminate, directly or indirectly, in a way that would exclude people of a particular race or sex from being selected.

The Part-time Workers (Prevention of Less Favourable Treatment) Regulations 2000 specify that part-time workers are entitled to the same statutory rights as full-time workers. They are also entitled to the same type of contract: permanent, temporary or fixed term. Some of the areas this should cover are:

- the name of your company and the name of the employee;
- the date when employment commenced;
- whether any previous employment affects the employee's continuous employment;
- the title of the job the employee is to hold;
- hours of work;
- details of pay;
- policy in the case of illness or absence from work;
- how often the employee will be paid (monthly, weekly?);
- details of holidays;
- details of any pension arrangements;
- grievance procedures;
- disciplinary procedures;
- notice required on either side in the case where employment is to be terminated.

Not all these headings need apply in your case. Under those that are to have no particulars, this must be stated.

A 'New Employer's Starter Pack' can be obtained from your tax office. It will contain all the forms and instructions you will need to operate PAYE (Pay As You Earn), as you will be obliged to deduct tax and National Insurance (NI) contributions from your employees' pay. The pack also explains Statutory Maternity Pay and Statutory Sick Pay. If you employ someone for only a few hours a week, they may be earning less than the figure at which such deductions start, so there would be less administrative work for you to do.

It may be that you would only need input from others on an occasional or sporadic basis, or that you have no wish to embroil yourself in the commitments that an employer must make.

alternatives to employing people

If you employ temporary staff from an agency, you just pay the agency fee and they sort out the tax and NI.

Depending on the industry you are in, subcontracting work out might be a better route. The construction industry uses this method extensively. The advantages are that you do not bear the administration costs of PAYE and NI payments, as you do in the case of an employee. Nor do you have a long-term commitment to someone whom you are using as a sub-contractor.

Under the Inland Revenue's Construction Industry Scheme (CIS), subcontractors (who can also act as contractors) must hold either a Registration Card or a Subcontractor's Tax Certificate. The first can be applied for immediately on trading and is known as a CIS4. The second is issued subject to certain qualifying conditions, mainly involving turnover, and will be a CIS5 or CIS6 depending on circumstances. This excludes you from having to pay tax at source when you subcontract to another firm.

choosing the right employee

As with advisers, it is better to interview a number of applicants for the job vacancy so as to find someone you feel you can get along with and trust.

You will need to define the job precisely so that the kind of experience and qualifications required are clearly outlined. There is no legal requirement to provide an employee specification, but where any such specification is provided, it must be clear that experience and qualifications sought are justified and not based on discrimination against sex or race.

At the interview it is better to withhold anything but a broad outline of the job so that the interviewee can be asked to express what their concept of the job is, why they want it in particular, and how they feel they are qualified to meet it.

You are making a decision that will affect you and your business over the short, medium and long term. Take all the precautions you can to help make your decision as near right as it can be. Such precautions might involve:

- ■ Having someone whose opinion you respect sit in on the interviews, even if only as an observer.
- ■ Holding more than just one interview with the applicant, shortlisting the best three or so for a second interview.
- ■ Obtaining references by phone. People will let slip more than they would in writing, and you can ask more questions than a written reference could answer.
- ■ Asking the applicant to apply their expertise specifically to the job you are offering in some measurable way. This could mean designing a logo, writing an article, taking a typing test or, as I was asked to do once, selling a pen to the interviewer. It depends on the nature of the vacancy whether such a test could be done on the spot, or would need to be prepared and sent in advance.

A free Internet Web site to guide small businesses through the maze of employment law can be found at www.emplaw.co.uk. The service is not intended to replace proper legal advice.

insurance

The additional area of insurance you will need to look at, aside from any insurance on buildings, contents and public liability, is employer's liability insurance. A certificate stating that you hold this must be displayed where it can be seen.

Many insurance companies offer a package of policies that cover most of the needs of a small business, but if you do opt to purchase this kind of package, make certain that each particular need of your company is catered for. Your own trade association, if you have one, may offer a comprehensive insurance package.

Insurance Advice for Small Businesses is produced by the Association of British Insurers (ABI) and is available free from the ABI by writing to 51 Gresham Street, London EC2V 7HQ or telephoning them on 020 7600 3333 or you could access their Web site, www.abi.org.uk.

summary

The Department of Trade and Industry's (DTI's) Small Business Service statistics show that at the start of this millennium there were 3.7 million businesses trading. Nearly 2.6 million were sole proprietorships and small partnerships. The same source shows that at least 95 per cent of businesses in all but the electricity, gas and water supply sector were small or medium-sized enterprises (SMEs). You've heard it before but now you know it's true: small businesses really are the lifeblood of the economy and, hopefully, you're about to be a part of that.

This book has suggested principles and given guidelines that should prove helpful and constructive. If there is to be a final word of advice it would be to continually update the information and data on which you base your decisions. The business world is ever-changing, and you will need to keep in step. It only remains for me to wish you every success in your new enterprise. Fortune favours the brave but more so if they have a business plan.

sources of further information

The following addresses may prove useful but the list is not exhaustive. Add your local agencies to it.

Association of British Credit Unions Ltd (ABCUL)
Holyoake House
Hanover Street
Manchester M60 0AS
Tel: 0161 832 3694
www.abcul.org

Association of British Insurers
51–55 Gresham Street
London EC2V 7HQ
Tel: 020 7600 3333
www.abi.org.uk

The British Chambers of Commerce
Manning House
22 Carlisle Place
London SW1P 1JA
Tel: 020 7565 2000
www.britishchambers.org.uk

British Franchise Association Ltd
Thames View
Newtown Road
Henley-on-Thames
Oxfordshire RG9 1HG
Tel: 01491 578050
www.british-franchise.co.uk

British Venture Capital Association
Essex House
12–13 Essex Street
London WC2R 3AA
Tel: 020 7240 3846
www.bvca.co.uk

Business in the Community (BIC)
131 Shepherdess Walk
London N1 7RQ
Tel: 0870 600 2482
www.bitc.org.uk

Chartered Management Institute
Small Firms Information Service
Management House
Cottingham Road
Corby
Northamptonshire NN17 1TT
Tel: 01536 204222
www.managers.org.uk

Companies House
Crown Way
Cardiff CF14 3UZ
Tel: 0870 333 3636
www.companies-house.gov.uk

Confederation of British Industry (CBI)
Centre Point
103 New Oxford Street
London WC1A 1DU
Tel: 020 7379 7400
www.cbi.org.uk

Direct Selling Association
29 Floral Street
London WC2E 9DP
Tel: 020 7497 1234
www.dsa.org.uk

Department of Trade and Industry
General Enquiry Unit
Tel: 020 7215 5000
www.dti.gov.uk

Everywoman Ltd
12 Hurlingham Business Park
Sulivan Road
London SW6 3DU
Tel: 0870 746 1800
www.everywoman.co.uk

Federation of Small Businesses
Sir Frank Whittle Way
Blackpool Business Park
Blackpool
Lancashire FY4 2FE
Tel: 01253 336000
www.fsb.co.uk

The Financial Ombudsman
PO Box 4
South Quay Plaza
183 Marsh Wall
London E14 9SR
Tel: 0845 080 1800
www.financial-ombudsman.org.uk

The Forum of Private Business
Ruskin Chambers
Drury Lane
Knutsford
Cheshire WA16 6HA
Tel: 01565 634468
www.fpb.co.uk

Franchise Development Services
Franchise House
56 Surrey Street
Norwich NR1 3DF
Tel: 01603 620301
www.franchise-group.com

Highlands and Islands Enterprise
Cowan House
Inverness Retail and Business Park
Inverness IV2 7GF
Tel: 01463 234171
www.hie.co.uk

Industrial Common Ownership Movement
Holyoake House
Hanover Street
Manchester M60 0AS
Tel: 0161 246 2959

The Information Commissioner
Wycliffe House
Water Lane
Wilmslow
Cheshire SK9 5AF
Tel: 01625 545745
www.dataprotection.gov.uk

Invest Northern Ireland
Tel: 028 9023 9090
www.investni.com

Office for National Statistics
Government Buildings
Cardiff Road
Newport
Gwent NP10 8XG
Tel: 01633 815696
www.statistics.gov.uk

Office of Fair Trading (OFT)
Fleetbank House
2–6 Salisbury Square
London EC4Y 8JX
Tel: 020 7211 8800
www.oft.gov.uk

OwnBase
(for homeworkers)
Birchwood
Hill Road South
Frodsham
Helsby
Cheshire WA6 9PT
Tel: 01928 723254
www.ownbase.com

The Prince's Youth Business Trust
18 Park Square East
London NW1 4LH
Tel: 020 7543 1234
www.princes-trust.org.uk

Scottish Enterprise, Edinburgh and Lothian
Apex House
99 Haymarket Terrace
Edinburgh EH12 5HD
Tel: 0131 313 4000
www.scotent.co.uk

Small Business Bureau Ltd
Curzon House
Church Road
Windlesham
Surrey GU20 6BH
Tel: 01276 452010/452020
www.smallbusiness.org.uk

The Telecottage Association (TCA)
Freeport CV 2312
Wren
Kenilworth
Warwickshire CV8 2BR
Tel: 0800 616 008
www.tca.org.uk

Welsh Development Agency
QED Centre
Main Avenue
Treforest
Mid Glamorgan CF37 5YR
Tel: 01443 845500
www.wda.co.uk

Women into Business
c/o Small Business Bureau Ltd
address listed above

directories

A Directory of Sources of Venture Capital under £250,000,
The Stationery Office, Web site enquiries on
www.hmso.gov.uk

Through the Web you can access an endless supply of information on sites such as Microsoft's www.bcentral.co.uk

The Kogan Page Creating Success series

Be Positive, 2nd edition, by Phil Clements
Be Your Own Boss, 3rd edition, by David McMullan
Better Business Writing by Timothy R V Foster
Boost Your Self-Esteem by John Caunt
Build Your Personal Brand by Eleri Sampson
Business Etiquette, 2nd edition, by David Robinson
Communication at Work by Judith Taylor
Dealing With Difficult People by Roy Lilley
Develop Your Assertiveness, 2nd edition, by Sue Bishop
Develop Your NLP Skills, 2nd edition, by Andrew Bradbury
Developing Your Staff by Patrick Forsyth
E-Business Essentials by Matt Haig
The Effective Leader by Rupert Eales-White
Empowering People, 2nd edition, by Jane Smith
How to Beat Your Competitors, 2nd edition, by John G Fisher
How to Generate Great Ideas, 2nd edition, by Barrie Hawkins
How to Manage Meetings by Alan Barker
How to Manage Organizational Change, 2nd edition, by D E Hussey
How to Motivate People by Patrick Forsyth
How to Negotiate Effectively by David Oliver
How to Run a Successful Conference, 2nd edition, by John G Fisher
How to Write a Business Plan by Brian Finch
How to Write a Marketing Plan, 2nd edition, by John Westwood
Improve Your Communication Skills by Alan Barker
Improving Employee Performance by Nigel Harrison
Make Every Minute Count, 3rd edition, by Marion E Hayes
Make That Call!, 2nd edition, by Iain Maitland
Making Innovation Happen by Michael Morgan
Organise Yourself by John Caunt
Performance Appraisals by Bob Havard
Stay Confident by John Caunt
Successful Presentation Skills, 2nd edition, by Andrew Bradbury
Successful Project Management by Trevor Young
Taking Minutes of Meetings by Joanna Gutmann
Team Building, 3rd edition, by Robert B Maddux
Using the Internet Faster and Smarter by Brooke Broadbent
Write That Letter!, 2nd edition, by Iain Maitland
Writing Effective E-mail by Nancy Flynn and Tom Flynn